Opening Windows to Change
a case study of sustained international development

Opening Windows to Change
a case study of sustained international development

Edited by JOHN SAYER

Oxford Studies in Comparative Education
Series Editor: David Phillips

SYMPOSIUM
BOOKS

Symposium Books
PO Box 65, Wallingford, Oxford OX10 0YG, United Kingdom
www.symposium-books.co.uk

Published in the United Kingdom, 2002

ISBN 1 873927 24 X

This publication is also available on a subscription basis
as Volume 11(1) of *Oxford Studies in Comparative Education*
(ISSN 0961-2149)

Typeset in Melior by Symposium Books
Printed and bound in the United Kingdom by Biddles Ltd, *www.biddles.co.uk*

Contents

Preface

Perm is a city of 1 million people in a region of 3 million across an area larger than the whole UK put together, some 2000 km north-north-east of Moscow, 2 hours behind on the clock, 24 hours by train, on the edge of the Urals. It was a closed city, opened up in the Gorbachov period, visited by Oxford academics and then linked more formally.

The joint projects used in this book as an evaluatory case study arose from personal Oxford-Perm links in which Andrei Kolesnikov played a key role. The title of the book is a reminder of the comment of the now Deputy Governor of the Perm Region, Tatyana Margolina, who thanked Andrei at the concluding meeting of our first project, for 'opening windows to the West'. It will be seen that the opening of windows has been in both directions.

The European Union's TEMPUS programme (trans-European Mobility Programme for University Studies), from 1990, was part, first, of its 'PHARE' technical aid for non-Soviet Union central and eastern European countries at the collapse of the Iron Curtain (Sayer, 1995a, 1995b), then also, from 1993, of its similar 'TACIS' response to the Confederation of Independent States emerging from the USSR (Sayer, 1995a). TEMPUS is the European Community's instrument for developing and restructuring higher education in both PHARE and TACIS-eligible countries. Both TEMPUS schemes are developed more or less on the model of the ERASMUS (European Action Scheme for the Mobility of European Students) programmes, which were focused on university cooperation and exchange within the European Community and now European Union (EU), though also permitting involvement of universities in G24 countries.

The TEMPUS symposium to the European Conference on Educational Research, held in Edinburgh in September 2000, was intended as a reflective, post-project evaluation of the development programme to prepare teachers to meet special educational needs (SEN) in Perm, and its continuation, extension, dissemination and effects on new related international work, including the follow-on TEMPUS-TACIS project for health education also featured here, Through this resulting book, the project can be seen as a case study for educational development programmes generally, for issues related to trans-European cooperation in education, for questions related to accountability, and for the relationship of development and research programmes.

The introductory chapter alludes briefly to EU TEMPUS programmes, in particular, the TEMPUS-TACIS programme and the contemporary Russian context. It offers a formal report of the special educational needs international project in Perm, which may be measured against the subsequent reflective chapters. It also records the EU/TACIS evaluations of the project. One purpose of the book is to show that such instruments of evaluation, however positive, as in this case, are inadequate for anything much more than minimalist accountability, which at the same time is in danger of stifling what is abidingly worthwhile in educational development.

The two following chapters in Part One are examples of reflective self-evaluation in the latter stages and after the formal conclusion of the TEMPUS project. During the preparatory year of the project, the joint management group from Perm, Amsterdam, Halle and Oxford agreed that a semi-detached group would be convened for constant self-review to inform the progress of the project. Its work included much more than the summative study recorded here: fact-finding, needs and situation analysis by researchers from Halle transformed initial assumptions; joint exploration early in the project by groups from Perm and the other partner universities resulted in shared writing, some of it published both in Russian (Kolesnikov et al, 1999; Charniy et al, 1999) and in English (van der Wolf & Sayer, 1999; Sayer, 1999); and the city and regional authorities were engaged in and have published parallel development studies in the context of new federal and regional legislation.

'Voices on Inclusion', by David Martin & Kees van der Wolf, is drawn largely from the evaluatory work of a colleague associated first with Oxford and then with Amsterdam. It is complemented here by the chapter from a Perm teacher-interpreter, Anna Popova, drawn by the project to advanced study in Oxford. The windows are opened from both directions. What both studies do is to probe beyond the formal account and to record what is happening where it matters most, in the hearts and minds of the main actors, in this case the teachers and trainers.

Part Two relates the TEMPUS project to wider conditions for change in schools. It is too often assumed that such development projects involve partners in stable situations, offering possible models for a target beneficiary in transitional need and search of new anchorage. But all of us are in constant change, whether because of new thinking, new priorities, new technologies or societal upheavals. East Germany, in particular, brings to the project its own dramatic experience of collapse and reconstruction. The chapter from Hartmut Wenzel & Gudrun Meister, itself a collaboration between academics drawn from two formerly confronting German societies, explores key elements of teacher experience before and after the German *Wende*, and illustrates the importance of teacher commitment to new approaches. It also adds a further dimension to the studies of East Germany in two recent issues of this series (McLeish & Phillips, 1998; Phillips, 2000). Ines Budnik with Hartmut Wenzel considers lessons to be learnt from our project to identify general principles for change. In both Halle contributions, the particular perspectives are of participants from an East German university which had experience of Soviet influence and has been undergoing similar societal, ideological and scientific change over the last decade. Academic, political, economic, cultural/historical, structural/organisational and personal dimensions of the transformation process are brought to bear on the project, and from this experience are drawn principles of joint international work.

A leading Russian exponent of new technologies for education, Evgeni Khenner, who has also supervised software developments in the Perm project, provides, with A.V. Kniazev, a succinct outline of the place of new technologies in change processes and outlines the history and current scope of information and communications technology (ICT) in Russian schools. Despite the starkly different starting points, they concludes that the role of ICT in Russian school development is essentially the same as in west European countries.

One test of the impact of a development programme is what survives after its formal conclusion, what it has triggered and enabled, whether change is from one static situation to another or whether change has become a part of institutional life. Although TEMPUS projects are increasingly measured and judged by somewhat limited and potentially limiting criteria drawn from outmoded and mechanistic management by objectives – these, of course, have to be complied with too – change engenders further changes unpredictable at the start of a process. So, Part Three gives space to examples of further exploration prompted by and outside the initial scope of a proposal. Home-school collaboration emerged during the TEMPUS programme as a priority, and it has been taken further by Andrea Laczik as part of a study across Perm and Hungary, as both accord greater recognition to parental rights and shared responsibilities for the education of their children. Similarly, during the special needs project, there emerged issues of pupil motivation and the effects of emotional stress and ill health on capacity to cope with curricular demands. The first issue has brought together four young researchers from Perm and Amsterdam, supported by Dutch government bursaries. The second has prompted a further TEMPUS project on health education, in the same partnership, and this current activity is reported by Alastair White, drawn into the partnership as its new coordinator. At the same time, he explores the applicability of models for transition (McLeish, 1998), and this is taken up in the concluding chapter, which also confronts the accountability patterns now seen to be undermining real change in and from such projects.

John Sayer, Editor

John Sayer

References

Charniy, B., Nikitin, I. & Kolesnikov, A. (Eds) (1999) *Problemi obutchenija detej so spezialnymi obrazovatelnymi.* Perm: Perm State Pedagogical University.

Kolesnikov, A. & Sayer, J. (Eds) (1999) *Obutchenije detej so spezialnymi nushdami.* Perm: Perm State Pedagogical University.

McLeish, E.A. & Phillips, D. (1998) *Processes of Transition in Education Systems.* Oxford: Symposium Books.

Phillips, D. (2000) *Education in Germany since Unification.* Oxford: Symposium Books.

Sayer, J. (Ed.) (1995a) Experiences of European Programmes with Central and Eastern Europe, in D. Phillips (Ed.) (1995) *Aspects of Education and the European Union.* Wallingford: Triangle Books.

Sayer, J. (Ed.) (1995b) *Developing Schools for Democracy in Europe.* Wallingford: Triangle Books.

Sayer, J. (Ed.) (1999) *Preparing Teachers to Meet Special Educational Needs in Russia.* Leuven-Apeldoorn: Garant.

van der Wolf, J.C. & Sayer, J. (Eds) *Opening Schools for All.* Leuven-Apeldoorn: Garant.

TEMPUS in Perm

JOHN SAYER & ANDREI KOLESNIKOV

EU TEMPUS-TACIS Joint Educational Project 10126 Objectives

This was the first TEMPUS project in Perm. Its declared prime objective was to help the Pedagogical University, which trains 60% of the region's teachers, to provide a continuum of teacher training for SEN in the Perm region. This would require partnership in teacher development with the region, the city, the specialised services and the schools. It involves university self-development, restructuring, reskilling and reprogramming to support the education service and through it the needs of the community. It was intended to enable long-term change in the service provided by the University in preparing teachers to meet SEN.

Specifically, the TEMPUS project was to help create a new interdisciplinary special faculty and university-based development centre, to make available appropriate SEN training, information, resources and programmes for teachers in all sectors of education. It was to support the development of higher education special needs training and qualification for teachers, in keeping with the new policy of the Russian Federation and the published Perm regional policy. In these, the approach to SEN is consistent with the development of democratic processes and rights in civil society. Through its partnership, it would provide a trans-European context for these developments, giving access to study, training and consultancy across the partner universities, and to key literature and resources.

Actions

Joint activities steered by an extended management group for the project included the following:

systematic continuous review of needs and resources for SEN in and around Perm, and of needs and resources for training teachers and related services to meet these needs;

supporting the establishment of the appropriate organisation for a new faculty and interdisciplinary centre, and developing a resource bank of development materials, information and literature, including the means to disseminate trans-European examples of good practice;

validation of regular, appropriate evaluation included in each project activity;

reporting on the progress and outcomes of the joint educational project as a whole;

dissemination and publication;

contributing to university staff programmes for special needs;

supporting the introduction of specialised retraining for existing teachers and their future work as coordinators of staff development in schools; and

supporting the development of new SEN modules in the initial training of all new teachers.

The steering group in Perm has been strengthened by the positive participation at leadership level of the regional authorities. The excellent working relationship with the Perm City authorities has continued to be crucial to the project, and the region's authorities and teachers are now equally involved in the postgraduate diploma course. The continuing support of city and region in making major contributions to fees and part release from teaching duties has been particularly remarkable at a time when only the highest priorities could be funded in this way. This not only enables the project to develop effectively across its whole range of activities, but underwrites the determination of both the University and the public authorities to ensure that the initial benefits of the project can be sustained. The strong university cooperation with city and region is a key to success. The University is engaged at all levels, and the direct support and involvement of the Rector and Vice-Rectors, together with heads of education in city and region, continues to be highly valued.

The centre, opened in the second year of the project, now has staffing to give improved access and resource support to teachers and schools as well as university staff and students. Objectives have been met despite severe administrative and financial difficulties caused by the European Commission and its agency, the European Training Foundation (ETF), (the subject of a separate formal letter), and despite the financial situation in the Russian Federation. The joint management group has continued to promote joint study and investigation; the project has again been presented as a case study in international conferences, and has generated further book, chapter and article publications as part of its review and dissemination strategies.

The needs and situation analysis has been further refined and investigated, and is reported in the project's evaluatory review, in contributions from Halle to international conferences, in the latest book publications from Perm, and in individual studies. Teachers from pilot schools have been included in study visits, together with university staff and public education authority leaders, to compare their innovations with practice elsewhere, and have received training visits from partner schools and specialists to follow up coursework in the University. For the pilot schools in Perm, counterparts have been found in all three of the partner consortia, for exchange of good practice in whole school management of change, university-school collaboration, and staff development for coordinated policy and practice related to SEN.

The university resource centre for special needs has been formally opened and has attracted regional and national attention. The centre is located and resourced to encourage maximum access for serving teachers as well as staff and students in the University. Two phases of equipment have been completed, and the centre is now well equipped for multimedia development. The involvement of the Professor for Information Technology, linking with the region's technology centre and the new university for information technology, is a key part of the project, and a team has been developing educational software for special needs. The University is engaged at all levels, and the direct support and involvement of the Rector and two Vice-Rectors continues to be highly valued. The project has encouraged a survey of practice across faculties which has identified that an element of teaching related to SEN is now a part of the experience of all those undertaking initial teacher training. With the resource provided by the project and inputs from its tutor team, there is evidence from some faculties that these elements have become increasingly practically oriented.

The resource centre has been additionally staffed, to improve access, and provided with three annual phases of equipment and resources. Summary translations of international texts have been further developed, equipment is now in place for multimedia work, and the team established by the Professor for Information Technology, linking with the region's technology centre and the new university for information technology, continues to develop software for work with children having SEN.

Training Programmes and Activities

The training team, drawn from different specialisms, and involving university lecturers with specialists working across the education and diagnostic service, has continued to review and develop its work on the 1-year post-service diploma programme. Its membership has been extended to cope with the additional numbers since the project's second year, and more have been drawn into the university orbit. They have shared in further intensive study visits and once again in the most recent evaluatory publication. The team is excellently assisted by the centre administrator, now having a resource assistant and technical support in the project centre.

The postgraduate diploma has been very positively reviewed by both the initial selected group of serving teachers, and the following cohort, including those drawn from the three designated pilot schools, all of whose leaders have continued to offer strong support. Follow-up school development work has included linkages with schools and universities in the partner countries, and these have been extended in all three EU partner countries.

Follow-up work is continuing with the initial selected group of serving teachers at their strong request. The intention to use the skills developed in the pilot and second cohort programmes not just for individual staff development but also for whole school development is reflected in the work being done on school development plans, which has been the focus of a series of study visits and consultancies in the second and third years of the project.

Family education is a priority for city and region; both are aware of parents' desire for normal schooling, and both are seeking to develop processes of management and policy, as well as direct work with children, and to share experiences of different countries. Examples of integration include physically handicapped pupils.

Despite a lower budget level and delays in producing both tranches of finances, the level of international mobility flows has more than matched the declared objectives. The visits from Perm have maintained the high standard of preparation and follow up and there has been no 'academic tourism'. The more restricted mobility visits from West to East have been equally effective, in joint survey work and 'action research' consultancy, continuing to develop shared understandings and addressing the key issues of teacher attitude, motivation, values and the bringing together of individual and project aspirations, and also contributing to the development of uses of information technology and of appropriate software. Some of the outcomes are to be seen in the project evaluation team's report.

Across all these areas of activity, there has continued to be very careful selection for East-West mobility visits, by the Perm coordinator in consultation with the project coordinator, of those likely to make a maximum contribution. As in the first two years, each visit has been preceded by a negotiated set of desired priority outcomes and has been followed up by reports to the Perm project team, including the city or region education office, and by written feedback. When necessary, groups have been accompanied by a team member who can at the same time act as interpreter and be involved in the translation of texts for the resource centre and for the joint publications. Some of the interpreters have become active contributors to the team, and five have been awarded scholarships for extended study beyond the project but in some cases directly related to it, in EU partner universities.

The role of EU partners in training has continued to combine study and training in visits to the EU, and to use a consultancy mode with small groups and individuals in training visits to Perm. The emphasis has been on staff, organisational and resource development, on the management of change, and on the exchange of good practice in helping children with specific learning difficulties.

The 1-year diploma programme is in strong demand. The second cohort of teachers drawn from the city has completed the programme, and teachers in the region have embarked on a parallel programme. It is already recognised in the field of social pedagogy, and successful completion of the course enhances the qualifications and remuneration of serving teachers. The additional 3-year course for non-graduate teachers, promoted by the project, is now firmly established with the benefit of the existing staff team and resources, and formal national recognition of the University's contribution to SEN has already been accorded at one level and is expected on a broader basis. Short courses have continued both in the University and across the city and region schools and districts. Course details for a sample year have been as follows:

1. One-year postgraduate diploma for mainstream school teachers from the city, completed in June 1999: 21 course members.
2. One-year postgraduate diploma for SEN school teachers from the city, started November 1998: 24 members.
3. One-year postgraduate diploma for SEN school teachers from the region, started December 1999: 17 members.
4. Four-year qualification for pre-school SEN, started November 1998: 22 members.
5. One-year qualification course for speech therapy: 22 school, 26 pre-school members.
6. One-year speech therapy course for students and practical workers: 21 members.
7. Courses for school headteachers: 2 months: October-December. 3 programmes. Total: 123 course members.
8. Regular seminar on rehabilitation of children with SEN: 23 members.
9. Seminar for technology teachers from special institutions: 23 members.
10. Seminar on mathematics for children with SEN: 16 members.
11. Seminar on Russian language teaching for children with SEN: 19 members.

Resource Development

Training materials continue to be developed and made available in the project centre: course materials have been developed as a resource bank. Progress has been made on accumulating key up-to-date books, and on providing a summary translation for key texts, both for the course members and for teaching staff. With the final project purchase of equipment, the centre is now in a position to produce more materials of high quality on site, and additional staffing has been funded.

The institutional development of the Perm State Pedagogical University is at the heart of the project. Team members for the project have been drawn from different departments, institutes and faculties to form a deliberately interdisciplinary approach to special needs. The linking of academic and professional strengths is assured by the ever-closer involvement in the team of practising psychologists drawn from the City Diagnostic Centre, from schools, and more recently, from those who have completed the 1-year course.. The extension of the Institute of Continuing Education for this project has given scope for joint university/city/region resourcing of the project, and has marked a strong development of the institution not only internally but in its external relations. The establishment in a central location of the University of a resource and training centre for serving teachers is at the same time an example of the university role in continuing professional development for teachers at all levels in the field. A new licence for work related to SEN in pre-school years has been awarded by the Ministry, and a 3-year course is under way, with the support of the project.

Good progress has been made on all fronts, and despite external obstacles, the stated objectives of the project were realised by the end of the third year. This included the objective of ensuring that the achievements of the project are sustainable and that measures are in place to ensure their continuation and consolidation.

The project has exposed one major element and cause of SEN which is a growing cause of concern in Perm. This is the health of children and its effects on educational achievement. Statistics in and beyond the project have shown a steady rise in such disabilities among young children, growing up in a heavily polluted environment. In order to confront this particular problem, a new TEMPUS-TACIS project has been proposed by the present partnership and accepted as JEP 10830 for 2000-2002, focused on teacher training and health education in the community, end-on to the current project, and this will build on the good working relationships and achievements already established, as well as enriching the contacts with which to sustain the present project.

The established management structure has continued into the new project, with a measure of continuity in modes of administration, communication, resourcing and personnel, and the symposium delivered to the European Conference on Educational Research at Edinburgh in

September 2000 recorded also the transition and cooperation across the two projects.

Making Links

There has been cross-fertilisation with a 'SOCRATES' programme on professional development materials for teachers in special schools, involving schools near Oxford and Amsterdam; as part of her training in evaluation, the Perm team member in Oxford carried out an evaluatory investigation and produced a report on the use made by three local special schools of the European curriculum materials developed in the SOCRATES programme.

A significant element of linkage has continued with the earlier TEMPUS-PHARE project on developing interprofessional training across services in Krakow, Poland. The arrangements made in that project for publications have been adapted for JEP 10216, and the Leuven contact, Johan Vanderhoeven, has kindly assisted with editing. Follow-up links made in that project between Halle and Krakow, Leuven and Krakow, Halle and Oxford have continued to be serviced by the management of JEP 10216. The distribution of the project's Russian and English publications to several such projects and other agencies was completed in summer 2000, and it is intended that this should lead to purposeful continuing liaison.

Liaison has continued with the Oxford-Perm Association. This link, first through individual and voluntary initiatives, then through the Oxfordshire Council for Voluntary Action (OCVA), and later through formal local authority linkage, has contributed to help for disabled people of all ages. Its work has included provision of wheelchair and other physical aids, support for the Youth Palace, which is now a learning centre for the disabled, and the setting up of a public advisory centre for the disabled. TEMPUS mobility visitors have assisted with communication and transport of gifts. There have been contacts with the TACIS-funded project in Perm directed by the Oxfordshire Council for Voluntary Action, and these have been reported at joint meetings both in Oxford and in Perm through the Oxford-Perm Association. Exchange visits by the mayors of both cities have included linkage with this project.

Problems and Solutions

There have been external problems, to which solutions have had to be found. The project has had in the final year to confront new external problems, some of which have been considered unnecessary:

(a) The financial and economic situation in the Russian Federation since August 1998 continued to test the management skills of Perm colleagues, who have managed remarkably well. The solutions found would not have been possible without total personal trust across the partner universities' representatives.

(b) The decline in the value of the ECU and then Euro against the pound sterling and US dollar during the period of this project in effect reduced the purchasing power of the TEMPUS grant by about 20%, i.e. 100,000 Euros, since the bulk of expenditure was from the United Kingdom contractor or the Russian Federation recipient. Faced with the alternative of not meeting the project's objectives and the likelihood of having to expend much more from other sources than originally anticipated, we have insisted on carrying through the commitments to our Russian colleagues, and this has resulted in a considerable 'loss', to be met from other sources. The only real solution would be for all partner countries to have adopted the common currency.

(c) The organisational problems within the European Commission, between the Commission and the ETF as its agency, within the ETF and between the ETF and projects have caused unacceptable problems. These have been the subject of a separate formal representation on behalf of the joint management group to the ETF, made in the hope that the good management of projects will not again be placed at risk.

Achievements

Despite such hindrances, the overall project objectives have been achieved in large measure, during a period otherwise marked by turbulence and uncertainty. This has been confirmed by the TACIS monitoring team, which has recorded the project's good potential sustainability, good relationship with Perm local administration, and close cooperation of the joint management group.

A teacher training university which prepares 60% of the teachers in a region geographically the size of Britain and France combined has to develop strong working relationships with the city and the region which it serves. There are structural impediments, notably through the different loci of control and accountability: universities are controlled tightly and their faculties licensed by the Russian Federation, i.e. from Moscow at a distance of 2000 km, whilst schools are the responsibility of the region (through oblasts and rayons) and the city, with funding by decision of their duma (parliaments). The Institute of Social Pedagogy, however, is able to raise funds locally, and it is the support and funding by city and region which is seen to be crucial to the success and sustainability of this project. That 'external restructuring' in the working relationship of university, public authorities and schools has been most significant. Moreover, the successful piloting through this project of a new concept of SEN has been a necessary first stage towards recognition and licensing by Moscow, so that the new faculty has been established and works across existing faculties of the University, all of which contribute to special needs training. In effect, a way has been found to bridge across structures and systems, and this is an exemplar for other Russian universities seeking to work in the context of their communities.

It remains to be seen whether this example will be followed, but the two project symposia organised by the University in Perm, drawing in higher education and public authority bodies and representatives from the whole region and beyond, and disseminated through project papers, have laid a foundation for similar initiatives elsewhere. Two books on the project's shared thinking and development activity have been published in Russian, for dissemination in the region and through national networks, in parallel with the two books published in English.

The impact on the education systems of the city and region has been acknowledged as significant. The city has clarified its policy for inclusion in mainstream schools; it has as a result of the project brought together for the first time the divergent statistical bases on which educational and medical services have been previously operating separately; and, through recognition of the 1-year diploma course as a salaried additional qualification, both city and region have shared in the promotion of school developments as a result of the programme. Tuition fees and overheads for these programmes, it should be emphasised, are funded to the University as priority by the city and region, and this income-generating activity will continue. Project management skills have been deployed at the University not just internally, therefore, but in the negotiated leadership of a consortium across the University, public authorities and schools.

This positive impact of the project also led to the proposal for the further project awarded as TEMPUS-TACIS 10830, and there is no doubt that the success of JEP 10216, as evidenced by external as well as internal evaluators, has been a major factor in its acceptance.

The interactivity with higher education institutions in the EU has been very positive, in what was by background a closed city. As a result of the project, the Dutch Government has funded three university scholarships of 6 months for doctoral students from the Perm State Pedagogical University; another has been awarded a newly created Carfax Scholarship at the University of Oxford. Perm now contributes to research and development publications published in the EU (as well as in Russian from Perm) and has made significant inputs to major European university conferences. Doctoral work by EU graduates has continued to develop from the links made through the project.

These developments have also had a beneficial effect in the EU partner universities. Shared management, evaluation, development of materials, writing and publication have been positive opportunities for professional development. Departments and faculties within universities have been drawn into cooperative training activity, and links with schools and services have been strengthened. Despite current tensions between research and development, opportunities have been taken to relate the project development programme to current research, and to open it to research investigation. In addition to the project publications, conference papers and articles in academic and professional journals have been published in English and in German.

Sustainability

As confirmed by the TACIS evaluation, there is a strong probability that the project results will be sustained and extended. The international partnership will continue, not only through the new project, which continues with the same management structure, but through bilateral arrangements across the universities.

The leading position of the University in generating thinking and training on SEN across the city and region education services is firmly established; there are already many schools which have a designated member of staff trained to promote staff development in this field, with the support of the headteacher, and the public authorities are now committed to extending this practice. About 100 serving teachers have now gained this new qualification. Local evaluation of the programme has been very positive.

The involvement of school practitioners from the outset in the preparation of the course programme, the insistence of the project that course members bring a negotiated school development project into the 1-year course, and the response of the University to initial evaluations by pilot course members have ensured that the teaching is directly relevant to the client groups.

The teaching team for the University was selected from younger members identified across faculties and drawing on psychologists and practitioners with experience in the field. Contributions from the EU have been strong, but predominantly indirect, i.e. in extending the preparation and experience of the teaching team. Direct inputs from the EU have been designed to enhance but not to replace the core team's work. There is no danger that the team will not be able to sustain its work. What needs to be ensured is a continuation of international experience for them and for new members of the teaching team.

Most significantly, the funding of the 1-year diploma qualification has been by the city and region, allowing the TEMPUS programme to foster team and resource development and international perspectives. That funding by public authorities will continue. The public and professional recognition of the 1-year diploma qualification will continue (and continue to be sought after, the courses being oversubscribed).

Despite strong support from public authorities and headteachers, there remains the question: will the developments initiated through the course in preparing key workers for staff development in schools really extend through the schools? The project has recognised that this depends on the management of change in schools. Courses and consultancy have been given as part of the project by professors of education management, in development work with headteachers and with whole school staffs. But there is little experience in schools of giving or recognising responsibility for staff development to designated trained colleagues other than the headteacher, and there has been some lack of confidence expressed by teachers on the course that they will be able to fulfil the role of a school coordinator beyond the direct management of children's needs. One positive side of this is that course members have requested follow-up days, and the University has responded to their request. It is hoped that the work of the University in promoting more participative management practice in the pilot and other schools will be sustained through the new project, which will face the same questions.

Universities in the EU are increasingly expected to give priority to research, and are having to consider how best to relate research and development. The separation between research and development funding in the EU causes problems. It would be helpful to emphasise the advantages of securing a parallel research project among the joint educational project partners; universities should be encouraged to enter into research-based development projects, and to follow up development work with research. Equally, it is important for east European universities to be encouraged to engage in joint international research beyond the preparation of doctorate students.

We wish to place on record sincere appreciation of the work of the Perm State Pedagogical University, Martin-Luther Universität Halle-Wittenberg, the University of Amsterdam, and University of Oxford Department of Educational Studies, together with consortium partners in schools, public authorities and services in all four countries. The project has depended on their dedication, creativity, enthusiasm, confidence and mutual trust, which are the foundation for a common future.

Voices on Inclusion

DAVID MARTIN & KEES VAN DER WOLF

This chapter, developed from a paper presented at the European Conference on Educational Research, held in Edinburgh from 20 to 23 September 2000, is an outcome of a working partnership between universities in Russia, England, Germany and the Netherlands (TEMPUS/TACIS-project 10216). The universities were the University of Amsterdam, the Martin-Luther Universität Halle-Wittenberg, the University of Oxford and the State Pedagogical University of Perm.

During the project period, the participants had several exchanges, with, among other things, two educational conferences at the Perm State Pedagogical University (May 1998 and September 1999). An outcome of the exchanges was the development of a research programme for special education in Russia. A description of the development of the project can be found in Sayer (1999) and van der Wolf & Sayer (1999).

In this article, we shall discuss, firstly, the concept of inclusion. It will then be connected to international trends and to the implications for the Russian educational system. The goals and organisation of the Perm project will then be connected to this discussion. The methods by which data were collected will be described. Changes in attitudes and the perspective of teachers, university educators and policy-makers will be examined and discussed. Statements and comments from interviews with participants will illustrate these changes.

Inclusion versus Integration

Inclusion as a concept is fairly new. Its origins lie in its use approximately a decade ago in the USA (Ferguson, 1997). Since then, it has become one of the key features of discussion in the literature of special needs education. In a recent publication, Sebba & Sachdev (1997) make distinctions between inclusive and integrative education:

Inclusive education describes the process by which a school attempts to respond to all pupils as individuals by

> reconsidering and restructuring its curricular organisation and
> provision and allocating resources to enhance equality of
> opportunity. Through this process, the school builds its
> capacity to accept all pupils from the local community who
> wish to attend and, in so doing, reduces the need to exclude
> pupils. (p. 5)

This stresses the whole school nature of the concept and the demands of reconfiguring regular schooling. The building of an inclusive school community is to reconstruct whole school provision, not the provision for SEN students only.

Integration, on the other hand, is usually applied to groups of students with exceptional needs having access and placement in a mainstream or regular school setting. This does not emphasise the restructuring of the whole teaching/learning and other processes; rather, it recognises the need for individual programmes for these students. As Sebba & Sachdev (1999) note, 'The organisation and curricular provision for the rest of the school population remains essentially the same as it was prior to the "integrated" pupils' arrival' (p. 7).

Farrell (1997) sees provision for special needs in three different ways. The three types of provision he considers are: (i) full comprehensive neighbourhood provision; (ii) the provision of special schools which have outreach facilities – thus, some partial integration could take place, with the two systems of special and mainstream schooling being maintained; and (iii) the resiting of special schools on to mainstream campuses, with linkage between the two types of schooling, that is mainstream and special. It allows for students with different disabilities to get special help and supplementary resourcing when needed.

Salamanca

Salamanca and Governmental Initiatives

In 1994, representatives of 88 national governments and 25 international organisations concerned with education met in Salamanca, Spain, under the auspices of UNESCO. In the Salamanca Statement and Framework on Special Needs Education (Porter, 1997), five principles of children's rights are mentioned:

> 1. every child has a fundamental right to education, and must
> be given the opportunity to achieve and maintain an
> acceptable level of learning;
>
> 2. every child has unique characteristics, interests, abilities
> and learning needs;

3. educational systems should be designed and educational programmes implemented to take into account the wide diversity of these characteristics and needs;

4. those with special educational needs must have access to regular schools who should accommodate them within a child-centred pedagogy of meeting these needs;

5. regular schools with this inclusive orientation are the most effective means of combating discriminatory attitudes, creating welcoming communities, building an inclusive society, and achieving education for all; moreover, they provide an effective education to the majority of children and improve the efficiency and ultimately the cost-effectiveness of the entire educational system. (Dyson, 1997)

Russia and Salamanca

The Russian Federation 'Law on Special Education' (1996) gives support to the United Nations view of inclusion. It wishes to see schools and regions work towards this end. The 'Law on Special Education', whilst embracing inclusivity, reflects the general tenets of the Laws on Education 1992-1994. These Laws profess the basic premises of education policy to be:

humanistic values and the free development of personality;
integration of the social institutes of culture and education at the federal level; ethnic and regional culture can develop autonomously;
access to education for all;
the system fits individual needs, not individual needs fitting the system;
the system of education is secular;
varieties of learning and teaching are adopted, not just one type of transmissive style;
governance of education is of a democratic nature in which educational institutions should be autonomous.

These indicative principles were reinforced with the documents: Social Protection of Disabled People Family Code, and Regulations on Special (Corrective [1]) Education for Children with Special Needs. This documentation requested of regions and municipalities that they take into consideration different aspects of the life of 'handicapped' children and realise their different operational contexts, the viewpoints and the leverage of different stakeholders in the community.

The TEMPUS/TACIS Project

The prime objective of the TEMPUS-TACIS Education Project 10216, which brings together the University of Amsterdam, the Martin-Luther Universität Halle-Wittenberg, the University of Oxford and the State Pedagogical University of Perm, has been, as has been described earlier (van der Wolf & Sayer, 1999), to assist the University in developing its capability to provide a continuum of teacher training for special needs education in the Perm region. Activities considered to be of importance in the course programme included:

1. a systematic continuous review of the needs and resources of SEN in and around Perm, and of the needs and resources for training teachers and the related services to meet these needs;
2. creating a new focus, an interdisciplinary centre, and developing a resource bank of materials and information;
3. creating a means to disseminate trans-European examples of good practice;
4. developing university staff programmes for SEN;
5. specialised retraining for existing teachers and their future work as coordinators of staff development in schools; and
6. new SEN modules in the initial training of all new teachers.

The 'project research group' would focus on the agenda set by policy-makers in inclusivity and its realisation in the mind-set and training policies and operations of educational stakeholders at school and training university level.

Methodology

The research group focused on differences in the different stakeholders' opinions regarding the feasibility of the concept of inclusion in Russia. The development of thoughts and ideas of teachers, teacher educators and policy-makers on various themes was then reviewed. These developments will be described and discussed below.

The data on which these descriptions are based were mainly gathered by conducting semi-structured interviews with 35 teachers, eight university course teachers and three policy-makers on topics ranging from the nature of inclusivity to course structure and change. These interviews were conducted using interpreters from Perm University who had insight into special needs education. Most of the material contained in this article is based on these interviews plus a selection of primary and secondary sources from logbooks, laws and regulations. Research was conducted over a period of 4 years at various stages of the project. Of course, the research covered the project agenda, which emphasised preparing some teachers for implementing more integrated or inclusive classroom practices, and did not in any deep way tackle the change issues involved in the more systematic reform effort.

The New Programme at Perm State Pedagogical University

New courses for teacher training in special needs were organised against this background in 1996, with a revision of the Standard of Higher Professional Pedagogical Education, 1995. The new courses would include four basic units:

1. common cultural;
2. medical-biological;
3. educational/psychological;
4. specialist aspects.

The new full programme (1600 hours) planned for the TEMPUS-TACIS Education Project 10216 comprised four phases with obligatory area subjects:

teacher personality related subject group (90 hours);
medical subject group (176 hours);
psychological subject-group (414 hours);
pedagogical subject-group (920 hours).

Further details of the programme can be found in Sayer (1999).

Before starting these new courses, further evidence had been gained in Perm, using needs analysis, showing that only 19% of student teachers favoured some form of integration, and that of children with mild disabilities. Indeed, most felt that SEN children should be segregated from their peers. The suggestion that SEN students should be included and that regular teachers needed to review their attitudes was greeted, in the main, with bemusement or hostility (Kozhanskaya & Oslon, in van der Wolf & Sayer, 1999). Further probing deduced that little knowledge was translated into school practices from teachers attending the traditional courses. The courses were not necessarily grounded in school-based instructional practices.

Results

Changes in the Views of Policy-makers

At first, policy-makers' attitudes were influenced by a general acceptance of the need to arrange a more inclusive environment for schooling: not a fully-fledged inclusive system, but rather, a greater emphasis on the integration of some students from special environments into the mainstream.

> *Well, I have a number of things to take into account. I can say*
> *the financial, but of course my real feelings of what is best for*
> *the children. They should be working alongside other children.*
> *We also now have a Russian law. We actually had this idea*
> *before the law. We are glad that our ideas are the same as the*
> *Ministry's. ... We also pioneer Leading Schools where we try*
> *out new methods and ideas. We would wish to see*
> *experimental schools and an interchange of students and*
> *teachers between the special and mainstream schools.*

As the project progressed, the policy-makers became more aware of the strategic issues, not only the direction of inclusive policy. They saw the issue of inclusive policy as certainly not realisable in the short term and energies should probably be directed to better practice within the locations where SEN children were being educated. Links could be made for more children in corrective classes to move to the mainstream. Towards the end of the project, policy-makers were also considering issues of sustainability in school settings with regard to incentives and rewards for teaching children with disabilities. They were aware that finance had been stopped in Russia for teaching children with challenging behaviour and learning problems. Perhaps this might be restored in the future, although probably not on a federal level; rather, it would have to be at a regional level.

During the running of the course, the municipality announced that it would not only pay for the participants on the course but also, it was hoped, the participants would be rewarded with an extra payment on completion of the course. This should be coupled with enhanced status for an SEN teacher.

> *Many of the course participants received a formally higher*
> *status: they became the methodological specialist, were*
> *offered the post of vice-head or were given promotion.*

Towards the end of the project, the policy-makers came to the realisation that whilst the course helped individual teachers and individual classrooms, there was a need to find ways of influencing schools as organisations. Professional development was seen not only in terms of personal and professional capacity building, but actions were critically situated in institutional settings where whole school considerations needed to be taken into account. Thus, further structural adjustment would be looked at via rewards and incentives. The policy-makers realised that, whilst the course had been very successful, the municipality now needed to look at systems of school organisation which would support inclusion, and to this end they were considering the enactment of further frameworks.

Changes in the Views of University Teacher Educators

The university staff were used to the biological-medical perspective on 'handicapped' children. The university educators seemed particularly keen to understand current thinking and practice in the field of special education. There was a realisation, on their part, that they now worked in a different cultural context, demanding new ways of looking at SEN. Special needs children and disabilities had been conceptualised as deficit models or problems. But course tutors became aware that this could close feelings and minds to constructing other ways ahead.

> *You must remember, we have come, until recently, from a closed Soviet city status. Until recently, we did not know of the scientific advances in the field. Even more, the chance to look behind their thinking and to see the variety of approaches – it opened new doors.*

The university staff were impressed by the teacher-student relationships they observed in western European schools. This led them to consider developing a more therapeutic, humanistic approach to course construction.

> *In Russia, there is an unspoken law that children with disabilities only need doctors to treat them and tell them how to study and to learn. Yet in England I saw people with a musical education treating children with disabilities, playing different sporting activities with them and the children made good progress ... I think it important that I place students in special schools and that they do research work on topics in those schools. For example, when I go with students for the first time to special schools, I then think perhaps something will work. My students are not acquainted with such problems, they have never been to such schools and have never seen such children in schools like that. When you make links, you have results.*

> *We need to conduct in-service education, particularly for some teachers in corrective education classes where they do not know about the need for disabled children to have physical education classes. We need to educate teachers not to make their children afraid of them and pressurise them. The teacher educator must give a teacher the chance to work creatively and realise the importance of subjects like music, handicrafts and physical education.*

Part of the training courses were also seen to have importance, when given a comparative perspective, which allowed critical and reflective understandings to be considered:

It is very important that trainers work together to compare different kinds of systems. From the theory of systems, it is known that a system can be tested only in comparison with the other systems. That is why we can duplicate our efforts and reach each other's systems. We tend to concentrate our courses on the personality of leaders and I think we could do more about the question of culture in school. We lack time and we succumb to methods that can be a little rigid. We have not had the time to change everything slowly, to change the culture slowly as in the UK. But you cannot pressurise school directors. They are adult, they already have their own personality. We cannot destroy them and we cannot rebuild overnight and that is why we try to be very caring towards them.

Some of these reflections led to a reconsideration of the types of culture building required in schools and the types of methodologies needed for adult learners who already had a great deal of experience. Therefore, one of the changes that occurred, for instance, during the course was that participants became very keen on more experiential methodologies of learning. In consequence, students found it difficult where excessively didactic or factually based topics were delivered in transmissive mode. One university educator found it difficult to pursue her course topic because her method of teaching did not allow for the needs of the students. Therefore, her style and approach had to be rethought. It did lead the university educators to review, as well, their methods of assessing students' assignments.

It was no longer productive to use traditional methods of feedback, students wished to have alternative ways of being evaluated.

In response to questioning about changes, after running the course for a year, a university educator stated:

Yes, of course there are bits I would like to change. Sometimes a student comes on to the course with a rather poor knowledge of the area. The student and I cannot get a more profound understanding of the issues if they do not have some basic knowledge. There is a problem of the amount of time we have. For instance, I would like to address issues of fluent speech in children, but instead of that we have to spend time on things like physiology maybe ... I need more time to intensify certain aspects. The time needed would probably need a new course.

Sometimes the trigger for the involvement in the course was a personal one. Some university educators were left after their own schooling and upbringing with some painful reflections, a personal experience, which had left them feeling that it was hurtful to exclude certain children.

It is a great problem in Russia when such children are divided somehow from other children and they are in their special schools and they are not being prepared to lead a normal life as members of society. When I was small, when I studied at school from the fourth to ninth grade, I remember children with movement or illness problems and from another school children with problems of speech and language.

The children from the two specialised schools made friends with each other but the children from the normal schools treated them badly. It turned out that there were some fights, these children were seen as alien and bad for us. But I thought, how badly we treated them and how sometimes they might be more clever than us. Some of them had good marks in mathematics and Russian but they couldn't go for further education after special school. The only work they could get was very simple. These children, they are always in my mind.

Another reason that was given for the need to set up the new course had been the course leaders' recognition of the psychological health of the teacher of SEN children.

I did a lot of surveys – with the result that teachers of SEN children have a disposition to develop a greater risk of a nervous breakdown. These teachers, also, were often personally defamed or stigmatised in the system of education in our country. This gives these teachers quite a unique structure of personality. It develops features in these teachers that prevent them working in an appropriate way with these children ... Teachers who work with SEN children in schools are not considered to be good, professional teachers. It is not prestigious to work with children with SEN. The prestige of the teacher in Russia depends on the amount of knowledge their students get.

The university educator, realising that teachers had to implement new changes, felt, therefore, that the first issue had to be changing their attitudes and this would require a focus as much on affective learning as on cognitive. This can also be seen as a change in the context of a move towards a more humanistic approach. Indeed, the name of educators such as Carl Rogers was frequently mentioned.

Well, first of all, the main thing we work at is the psychological atmosphere and relationships between teachers and children. The attitude of teachers to their jobs and the attitude of children to education. We try to improve the level

> *of teaching and the new methods needed. Also, the*
> *expectations of children's achievements and the quality of*
> *education. Important also is the practical realisation of the*
> *idea of differentiating learning activities according to the*
> *needs of the child, their families and their abilities.*

The university educators carefully reviewed a more therapeutic approach and were very pleased when it proved to be productive and popular.

> *For the first time in Russia, a lot of attention has been paid in*
> *teacher training to personality development of the teacher and*
> *a positive attitude towards SEN children.*

It is worth noting that the course leaders themselves saw their work as 'personality training for SEN teachers' (van der Wolf & Sayer, 1999).

As has been mentioned previously, teacher educators were also interested in the changes needed by people brought up in a command, Soviet system. Some of the comments that follow reflect the strong cultural impact of this system and why the teacher educators wished to put a greater emphasis on self-awareness and self-assessment.

> *What we see is a stereotype of the person who can't change*
> *herself or her life or her circumstances. What we see usually is*
> *a person who sits and waits for somebody to force them to do*
> *something. But it is necessary for teachers to tell those in*
> *authority that they can change and can do something ... They*
> *can change things when they work as teams and I have been*
> *involved where there has been a union between the director of*
> *the school, her assistants and psychologists. We try to get*
> *schools to form teams. This is very important.*

A university educator in leadership studies said:

> *There is a problem that a person thinks that he is a democrat*
> *but he is an authoritarian in practice. We notice that if they*
> *are from an authoritarian tradition they seem to inhabit or are*
> *in a twilight psychological zone. We try to get the participants*
> *to look at ideal models of treatment of others and*
> *relationships and contrast this with their real way of thinking*
> *and their real way of acting. There is a real clash when these*
> *two models try to work together. People feel great*
> *psychological stress because they begin to understand that*
> *they want to be a democrat and in reality they are*
> *authoritarian. But the demonstration of this very conflict can*
> *lead to a change in their consciousness. But this change does*
> *not happen overnight, it takes time. He has to go through these*
> *problem conflict situations. We try to get the participants to*
> *understand the conflict within themselves, not just as one*

emanating from external powers or other teacher. Rather, the problem that worries him is that his work does not live up to what he should be doing. He must change himself to be himself ...

I noticed a change: the child was no longer a threat to them. Their attitude became changed over the year ... They returned to school full of enthusiasm about what they learnt on the course and very eager to introduce changes. But because of conditions at school sometimes the enthusiasm becomes less ñ there seems to be no room for development.

An interesting occurrence was that teachers who were participants on the course noticed changes in the children they were teaching. However, any innovations were not necessarily developed or could be developed in a deeper way in a school-wide setting. This led the university educator to review the impact of the course in terms of its effect in the school situation, because, whilst the course was developing the teacher personally and professionally, there was still the stereotyping and stigmatisation of the SEN teacher to be considered. Whilst the child in the classroom was no longer seen as a threat, some professional colleagues and the climate of the school could be seen in this way. The university educator therefore felt that there would need to be new courses to tackle the institutional issues involved in inclusion. The training for some of this was already being carried out in the leadership courses. However, there was still a need to tackle directly with teachers in schools professional development for integration.

Leaders of schools are a very specific group of people. The majority of them are teachers that have no education about organisations. When they become a director of a school, they have to deal with problems, for instance, over resources and supply of staff which they never have had to deal with before. They become transfixed by administration. That's why, for example, instead of dealing with educational processes, they deal with toilets. In time, difficulties and the mistakes they have experienced means they only deal with more instrumental administrative problems. They don't care about educational process, their assistant deals with this. So if a director finds a good assistant, the assistant is really the leader of the educational process. Unfortunately, the assistant may make mistakes because he is not a very good communicator or he hasn't enough knowledge to analyse the work of the teacher. It is difficult for him to build strategic programmes for the educational policy of the school. It is difficult for him to share things or delegate between his assistants or psychologists at school.

One of the main barriers to change, as the university educators perceived it, was the culture of the school.

> *The majority of our schools have a role culture. Everything seems rather limited and there is no movement and development. Some, of course, have command cultures where the director of the school is the king. Of course, if the king is kind then everything is OK and he is interested in new ideas and developing them. We would like to see schools with a special culture, a culture with an active or developmental aspect. We would like to see teachers form special groups, according to their interests or wishes or wants, to change some aspects of instruction in the school. In the course of time there is a leader who is in charge and can coordinate that activity. Well, in other words, it is a kind of correction to the status quo culture of the organisation.*

University teachers became very aware of the importance of taking into account organisational culture in the embedding of new ideas:

> *Sometimes change was very difficult because of the mentality of professional colleagues in schools. Then there is, of course, some financial problems and a lack of resources, rooms and equipment.*

In subsequent interviews at the end of the project, university tutors raised the following issues which would need to be considered in the course review:

1. schools may need some continual consulting system to help with a problem;
2. the need to develop different attitudes within a whole school environment;
3. their rigidity of timetable organisation;
4. the need for school directors to have training to support new initiatives;
5. the matching of personal and professional development in the context of institutional development; and
6. the necessity of developing an inclusive climate/ethos in schools.

They also felt that they still needed to focus on new plans for looking more closely at the classroom environment, which would become the site of integrated/inclusive practices.

Changes in the Views of the
Teachers Participating in the Project Course

Some initial thoughts from the teachers on the course concerned the backgrounds of students who might bring problems to the mainstream situation, but who also were seen as constituting a large proportion of students in special situations or corrective classes.

> *Another problem of including children is the difference of*
> *including children from our school who come from poor*
> *families. The problem between rich and poor will arise. These*
> *children will be unable to buy luxurious items that normal*
> *children have. Some things are very expensive; now being*
> *teenagers, some will have problems communicating with their*
> *parents. The parents have not enough money to buy them*
> *these things.*
>
> *[Question: And what happens when there are corrective*
> *classes?]*
>
> *Well, it is said that if one child from a problem family*
> *influences children from similar backgrounds, they then form*
> *gangs.*

Another teacher took up the issue of children's attitudes, reiterating that it was better if they could all be taught together:

> *The problem children, if they are in the same class, begin to*
> *imitate each other's bad behaviour and attitudes. Conversely,*
> *when they get a good example they also try and imitate those*
> *good behaviours.*

In general, there was agreement about the benefits as an ideal of inclusivity, but real fears about the number of variables militating against its achievement.

The New Programme

Russian special needs pedagogy (defectology) has had a strong medical orientation (Bailey, 1998). Much of the curriculum was on the working of the brain, the physical background to hearing and sight problems. A diagnostic, prescriptive approach was stressed. Before being admitted to special needs education, each child still has to be screened by a 'pedagogical and medical commission'; as well as representatives of the local government, others like a child psycho-neurologist, a psychologist, an infant defectologist, a speech therapist, an ear, nose and throat specialist and an ophthalmologist often serve as members of such a commission.

Initially, teachers felt that there needed to be further help in gaining understanding of the myriad of disabilities, according to the above-mentioned criteria. Thus, the teachers' view of this area was heavily influenced by these conceptions.

I was pleased that a sufficient amount of psychological
training was provided. I should like more attention to be paid
to neuro-psychology and to the medical aspect relating to the
attitude towards SEN children as well.

Most participants felt that the University and the teacher educator had a key role in developing the knowledge and understanding of the teacher in the area of special needs. They wished that they, as teachers, could, particularly, gain extra knowledge on disabilities and how these children could learn better, or be taught better in either special schools or corrective classes. They began to realise after a few weeks that whilst the course helped them professionally, there was, further to this, a change needed in their psychological outlook.

They were particularly pleased when the university teachers used non-didactic methods on the course. They liked to discuss issues, to reflect upon practice and were generally very positive about the use of dialogic methodologies. On the teaching methods used in the University, whilst participants enjoyed the lectures, which were seen as vital in some respects, they were really more impressed with the dialogic emphasis to problem-solving and active learning.

It is easier to acquire information in training sessions,
workshops, in groups and in practical lessons than in lectures.

The teaching methods are pleasant. The alternation of
lectures, training sessions and practical work prevents it from
being boring and it gives good results.

However, they also thought it was important to have lectures on particular topics. But one of the key issues about the lectures and other methodologies used was that they could be applied in their practice.

General ideas about the methodologies used were further reinforced as the course progressed. They felt that their understanding had improved greatly in the area of their own positive dispositions and classroom practice. However, they also became aware of areas that would need extension. The key issues about the role of the university educator were that they built upon the practitioners' desire to have their practical experience both valued and better informed. As one participant said, 'We do not mind theory; indeed, it is important, as long as practice prevails'.

Whilst, at first, some of the participants found it painful to have to examine their practices and motives, they felt that it had been a necessary and worthwhile experience to be taught in a more experiential manner. One teacher remarked that what was so important was that:

I felt I was learning personally, not just professionally. It even helped me, in dealing with my own child. I learnt new ways of soothing and calming him, without confrontation.

While attending classes, I became aware of how much I had lacked. I am used to teaching and assessing pupils' progress, but I still have to learn how to communicate with them 'at the level of feelings'. I have also realised how important it is to work with my pupils' parents.

Some of the participants learnt new methods of how to deal with children who were reluctant in the classroom, who would not do anything:

I was absolutely paralysed and I would not know what to do. I thought the fault was mine and I became irritated by the situation. I was not cruel to any child, but on the course, they told us how to overcome this sensation by soothing and caressing the child. I remember there was a young boy, who had been abandoned by his mother, who is now 13 years old and into drugs. I dealt with him in this new way, despite his deviant behaviour, and one day when leaving the class he said thank you because when I finished the class I also say thank you and thank you for your work.

The course participants liked the way they considered the child in a broader context, taking into account other viewpoints.

The contents of the course allow one to look at a student's problems from the point of view of a teacher, a psychologist, a pedagogue and a parent. One develops a problem-oriented approach to education of children. I feel that I should still like to go on learning for a while, that is to say: there are still questions left and enough chances for improvement.

The course helped me to see myself from another side and to see an SEN student from a different angle. It provided a scientific basis to intuitive action. My knowledge of many subjects has become broader.

One participant on the special education training course also learnt new methods of teaching which particularly targeted individual ways of teaching students. They also got information about how to identify children with special needs. They developed different activities and teaching strategies for children, for instance, using visual aids, whereas in the Soviet system they were taught in a highly organised, transmissive, command way. They were also pleased to learn new assessment activities from the social pedagogy teaching, which they could put into practice in their own classrooms.

The Comparative Experience

Many teachers from Perm schools visited England, Germany or Holland. They especially acquired information on policy and working methods in the different countries. Because of their educational history, it was difficult for them to understand that it was possible to include children with disabilities in the mainstream.

> *It was an exciting experience for us to visit Holland. It came as*
> *a shock to see the children with defects in normal classes.*
> *Most of these children would have been in boarding school*
> *and some not in school at all. Children with physical*
> *handicaps, in rural areas, did not go to school at all. We learnt*
> *a lot by seeing it, we did not believe it could happen.*

They particularly stressed the difference in the relationships between teachers and students. While they recognised that some teachers established relationships of care and reciprocity, many teachers still only had a command or transmissive mode of delivery. They were particularly impressed where they saw genuine interactional methodologies in practice. They were also very impressed by the fact that it was not just specialists but other teachers who taught these children.

There was very little mention of aspects of school organisation in the initial interviews. The teachers' main concerns were, firstly, their own personal changes in order to accommodate a more inclusive world view. Interviews at the end of the course showed much greater awareness of institutional issues. In a school which had already been experimenting in integrative practices, their main concerns became not structural: rather, the further development of relationships and methodologies of teaching/learning. With other teachers, there was frequent mention of the need for teamwork both within the school and with parents. They wished to get away from relationships based on command and fear. They also felt it imperative that heads understood the need for a supportive environment in order for the changes to work. Some went further and advocated more devolved decision-making structures of governance within the school.

Discussion

As with all courses which have been well received, this course expanded people's expectations, yet created further awareness about the constraints. With the curriculum content devised in the way it was, it led to many teachers feeling they had a greater control over their practice. The problem for them was sometimes the level of support received in the schools and the institutional problems encountered in either developing other people or changing the formal curriculum. One or two teachers felt that where they had been given support for the curriculum change, its realisation, in practice, took place in extra-curricular time. The issue of confronting new dimensions of curricular time within the normal timetable was not faced.

The issue that this raises is that this is an excellent course for starting the movement towards consciousness-raising and individual practices, both at a professional and personal level. However, the participants interviewed felt that there must be more emphasis in the curriculum on school change, management and professional development of teams. Of course, it may not be possible to achieve all those goals in this particular course, but like all good courses, it raises further questions about the length of course, type of course, and the relationship between research and enquiry and practical developmental goals.

Note

[1] By corrective education in the Russian system is meant special classes of students, withdrawn from the mainstream, in the first years of elementary education. The students had to do an extra year before entering the secondary phase.

References

Bailey, J. (1998) *Medical and Psychological Models in Special Needs Education*, in C. Clark, A. Dyson & A. Millward (Eds) *Theorising Special Education*, pp. 44-61. London: Routledge.

Dyson, A. (1997) Inclusive Education: a theoretical and comparative framework, paper presented to the European Conference on Educational Research, Frankfurt am Main, Germany, 24-27 September.

Farrell, P. (1997) *Teaching Pupils with Learning Difficulties: strategies and solutions*. London: Cassell.

Ferguson, D.L. (1997) How Systematic Are Our Systematic Reforms? in *Implementing Inclusive Education, OECD Proceedings*, pp. 49-55. Paris: Organisation for Economic Cooperation and Development, Centre for Educational Research and Innovation.

Porter, G.L. (1997) What We Know about School Inclusion, in *Implementing Inclusive Education, OECD Proceedings*, pp. 55-67. Paris: Organisation for Economic Cooperation and Development, Centre for Educational Research and Innovation.

Sayer, J. (Ed.) (1999) *Preparing Teachers to Meet Special Educational Needs in Russia*. Leuven-Apeldoorn: Garant.

Sebba, J. & Sachdev, D. (1997) *What Works in Inclusive Education?* Ilford: Barnado's.

van der Wolf, J.C. & Sayer, J. (Eds) *Opening Schools for All*. Leuven-Apeldoorn: Garant.

The Teacher Retraining Programme: a Russian evaluation

ANNA POPOVA

This chapter focuses on the TEMPUS-TACIS project 10216 in Perm, Russia, which helped organise and conduct a teacher retraining course for special educational needs. The impact of the course is evaluated through a series of interviews with course participants and project team members . Conclusions are drawn in a broader theoretical context of special education in Russia. The project has been completed with great success because it adopted a highly professional approach to activities and reached a high level of sustainability. Some of the project's developments have been hindered by cultural and contextual peculiarities in Russia. There is still a long way to go in changing educationists' thinking on inclusive education. However, the project itself has been skilfully run and lessons can be derived from it for similar projects.

Background information, such as the aims of the project and its phases, are described in detail in other chapters. An overall evaluation is presented in the chapter by David Martin & Kees van der Wolf. They, however, evaluated the project as a whole while I focused mainly on the views of participants.

Special Education in Russia, Past and Present

These peculiarities derive from the distant and more recent past of special education in Russia. Attitudes to the disabled and handicapped stem from a Christian orthodox approach: 'Do not forget about the unfortunate, feed them; do not let the powerful people offend them'. These words belong to Prince Vladimir Monomach, Russian Tsar in the twelfth century (Goneev, 1999). By the nineteenth century, the situation had changed. This period saw the foundation of social organisations responsible for the education and upbringing of children with disabilities. At this time, notable theorists emerged in this area, including E. Gracheva, N. Kaschenko, G. Rossolimo, G. Troshin, A. Lazurskiy, A. Vladimirskiy and N. Checkov. These and others were fighting against the conservatism of the Tsar's government over policies for the disabled. They insisted on reform in education and the health service. Despite a number of attempts to attract the state to the needs of the disabled, special education provision by the beginning of the twentieth century was still in the hands of charitable organisations only.

A new attitude to children with special needs began to evolve after the October Revolution. The care of children became the responsibility of the state. Disabled and disadvantaged children gained the right to education. The measures taken by the state were directed at eliminating homelessness and developing health awareness. The motto, 'All the children are the children of the state', typified policies of that time. This resulted in various decrees and legal acts adopted to improve the life of children and to protect motherhood and childhood.

Increasing numbers of special institutions were opened, selection being by a medical-psychological approach, largely based on the ideas of Vygotsky (1896-1943). In his theory of mental development, he advanced an important new notion called the zone of next development (ZND) (also translated as the 'Zone of Proximal Development'). This notion is central to Soviet-Russian understanding of what needs to be done for 'backward' or 'handicapped' children. Psychological research into the problems of teaching has usually been restricted to establishing a child's level of mental development. That level is usually defined by the problems that the child solves on their own, and this indicates the stage of development that the child has reached. However, any development involves transferring to a higher level of mental cognition. In children's development, this can be achieved by helping them to solve the problems that are meant for older children. Such help comes in the form of demonstration, a leading question, the start of the solution, etc. According to Vygotsky (1986, p. 56):

> *The zone of next development has more direct significance for the dynamics of mental development and school achievement than does the present level of children's development.*

Others have emphasised that Vygotsky's ZND offers a dialectical approach to assessing child development, regarding the individual child's development as the current but dynamic product of two processes, teaching and learning.

This theory provided a basis for the whole system of special education in the Soviet Union, and then in Russia. It states that children with disabilities can be divided into two major groups – children with oligophrenia and children with other forms of backwardness. Oligophrenes are children whose mental and academic retardation is caused by a disorder of the central nervous system that interferes with normal processes of learning and generalising. This disorder is irreversible and though, as with all handicapped children, enormous progress can be made with appropriate special educational help, oligophrenia imposes limits that can never be fully overcome. The result of such an approach is that, in Russia, there has appeared a great diversity of special schools which are classified according to the kind of disability children have, whilst in the UK, children are classified in a continuous manner as having 'mild', 'moderate' and 'severe' learning difficulties.

The lifting of the iron curtain damaged many stereotypes, values and structures. The Russian public and professionals realised what thirst they had for 'learning lessons from abroad' and sharing their experience. Not only the lessons seeped through, but also the whole international culture and ethos of protecting human rights, including children's rights, in developing education. Russia was obliged to engage in the activities of international organisations that promote worldwide strategies, and had a very tight time schedule to build on its educational history as well as develop new policies and approaches.

Generally, current policy-making in Russia is in line with humanistic development, a blend of all the tendencies described above and the new international movement. The Ministry of Education has elaborated clear directives that regulate admission of SEN children into special educational institutions (especially residential schools). Parental choice of an educational institution has been ensured by law. Now, parents may agree or disagree with the decision of the joint psychological, medical and pedagogical panel. Parents and children are offered a variety of options: special schools; corrective (remedial) classes; or classes of compensatory education (withdrawal from some lessons).

Greater attention to children with SEN generated new educational programmes for special schools with new forms of staffing – schools were provided with speech therapy, psychological and medical help. Perm has been very active in developing new local policies. In 1994, the Perm Department of Education launched a programme, 'Development of Special Education in Perm for 1995-2000', integral to the plan for stabilisation and development of education in the Perm region until the year 2000 (Goutnick, 1999).

The number of special schools in the Perm region is increasing. The number of children having SEN is growing owing to environmental and social problems, and the dominating philosophy is that different approaches should be applied to different kinds of disabilities. This requires special conditions – special schools. New types of institutions for SEN children are being opened (e.g. the Centre for the Rehabilitation of Orphans). Special schools are changing their profiles and developing vocational courses as well as links with vocational colleges. More efforts have gone into developing a special sector of education and fewer activities have focused on inclusion. The main reason for this is said to be an 'under-developed culture of attitudes towards people with special needs' (Goutnick, 1999).

The growth and development of special education in the Perm region involves both advantages and disadvantages for introducing inclusive policies into practice. Opening special services that support educational institutions, such as 16 speech therapy centres, is certainly of great help to the staff of mainstream schools. However, creating such biased courses as 'Foundations of Defectology' in one of the teacher training colleges in Perm is leading new specialists in the field back to the option of special education for SEN children.

Values – ideology change

The transitional period has created a stir in pedagogical thought. Seventy years of ideology-driven educational practices were reflected not only in numerous textbooks but also in *vospitanie* (upbringing) – considered in Russia to be the central element in a child's development. The pedagogical literature of the 1990s dwelt on the collapse of the old ideology and the need for a humanisation of education. According to Lutovinov & Poletaev (1998), there are new tendencies for developing a new ideology that might be called the ideology of state patriotism. This includes traditional and historical elements of Russian culture, the way of life and national customs. It also presents a synthesis of Russian thought and current and historical realities as well as social experience. Unfortunately, such an ideology is only in its early stages. For educationists, this means moving away from a well-defined and transparent path for education to one that is blurred and very unstable.

Educationists, in protest at the uniformity endured in the past, started promoting a diversity which has gradually turned into a system of uncontrolled freedoms. The new diversity has brought with it not only new freedoms but also chaos and misunderstanding in the work of teachers who cannot keep track of fast changes in policy. This situation has also been intensified by the traditional disrespect for the law (Alikina & Prakke, in van der Wolf & Sayer, 1999) that has deep roots in Russia. With regard to SEN, many schools in Perm, for example, do not know that striving for integration and inclusion is laid down in law.

A significant change in values is described by Bîrzea (1996) as a common feature for all societies in a transitional period. It is the time when material values prevail. The Russian people, previously renowned for a communal mentality, have developed by now an extremely individualised approach to life. Such a decline in values is especially dangerous for education, which is a financially profitable area. In these circumstances, there is a real risk that special education appears at the bottom of the priority list. That is why integration as a considerable shift in educational thinking could have been ignored; hence, the actions of the TEMPUS project to meet SEN in Perm.

Findings of the Research Interviews

Sixteen people were interviewed, among them mainstream and special school teachers, headteachers of pilot schools, coordinators and other members of the project team. The interviews were considered against the background of some theoretical considerations. According to the findings of the research, the TEMPUS-TACIS project was important in:

introducing a new idea of inclusion in a Russian context;
setting up a new type of teacher retraining course; working as an international project in the area of education; and
providing lessons for similar projects (see chapter 5).

Introducing a New Idea of Inclusion

Developments of inclusive education in Russia seem to be following a well-trodden path of some other countries. However, Russia has responded to the international movement towards 'education for all' rather later. The forces that restrict effective development of inclusion originate from the specialised medical approach that still predominates and the political and economic instability in Russia. Despite these problems, the project has achieved a significant breakthrough in the thinking of the educationists who have undertaken the retraining course.

A considerable change is discernible in teachers' thinking with regard to SEN students:

The project helped me realise that it is possible to work with such children (forgotten and abandoned by everybody), that in fact these children are very capable.

What the project managed to do is that it changed the attitude to children with SEN.

Teachers are aware of the implications inclusion can bring to schools; among them, the issue of 'non-acceptance' of children with SEN occupies a significant place:

What I am afraid of is that our children will be thrown into mainstream school when the mentality of other people is not ready to accept the difference. I am afraid that our children will be rejected in mainstream.

Inclusion versus segregation: change in attitudes. Most of the participants acknowledge there has been some shift towards integration. The shift is mostly described as a change in thinking from non-acceptance of children who are different from the majority. The change is generally felt at all levels – coordinators, headteachers and teachers. Special attention in all the interviews is paid to comparison between the past and the present, though sometimes the comparison is not aimed at describing the movement towards inclusive thinking. Some participants do not seem to realise that they have experienced some change, though this is implicit in their answers. They reflect on the change during the interviews and it is possible to glean what influence the course and the project had on their attitude towards SEN. Some of the answers are straightforward and show that change has taken place:

> *The aim of the course was to restructure the psychology*
> *(thinking) of teachers who work with children in corrective*
> *classes, because we do not know such children.*

> *The project helped me realise that it is possible to work with*
> *such children (forgotten and abandoned by everybody), that in*
> *fact these children are very capable.*

The significance of the change in attitudes and general educational approaches is more explicit in the answers given by managers and headteachers. They emphasise that educational thinking in Perm has made a huge step forward to an approach to SEN that is consistent with democratic processes and rights in civil society. In their answers, they express their personal opinion of the change in thinking and educational philosophy and base it on the experience of their work:

> *As a headteacher, I can see that though the major aim was to*
> *organise and manage education of SEN children, we have*
> *stepped over these limited aims and started developing new*
> *approaches to education of all children. The initial idea grew*
> *into health education and creating an environment that is*
> *psychologically comfortable not only for SEN children but for*
> *all children at school. We are looking now at developing an*
> *environment that forms values and that forms intellect.*

Arguments for and against a 'segregated' type of special education. Mainstream and special school teachers differ in their attitudes to segregation. Special school teachers, despite the influence of the project, which has afforded a different perspective, have a stronger belief that placing SEN children in special schools is more beneficial to them than leaving them in mainstream schools.

> *Mainstream schools lack the atmosphere of a special school*
> *where a child feels on the same level with other students.*
> *Nobody mocks or laughs and self-esteem grows.*

*Children get a vocation in our school, which would be
impossible in mainstream schools.*

Special school principals and teachers feel that they are very different
from mainstream teachers and therefore are very proud of understanding
what a disability is. They emphasise that mainstream teachers do not
possess enough knowledge to work with SEN children and really focus
on the disability of children in their school.

Throughout the interviews, special school teachers concentrated on
the particular difficulties they experienced in working with disabled
children. Those who work in special schools for intellectually disabled
children, defined in Russian terms as oligophrenes, emphasise that it is
much more difficult to work with them than with any other type of
students:

*I find it very difficult to work with intellectually disabled
children. Physically handicapped, children with poor sight or
hearing are different. It is much more difficult to work with
oligophrenes. We spend too much energy. It is amazing how
uncontrollable they are. Junior or senior – their behaviour is
outrageous!*

It is evident that segregation or closed special education is still regarded
as a solution to problems caused by disability. The idea penetrating all
the responses is that special provision which results in segregation is
supported by people's ignorance of what disabled people are like. What
is implied is that special schools protect children from misunderstanding
and inadequate treatment from people around them.

*What I am afraid of is that our children will be thrown into
mainstream school when the mentality of other people is not
ready to accept the difference. I am afraid that our children
will be rejected in mainstream.*

This does not mean that there is no compromise between mainstream
and special teachers to allow in the long term an inclusive approach in
education, but they do point to the huge gap between the current school
system and integration. The problem is complicated by the fact that
mainstream teachers complain about the lack of knowledge of special
school provision. Their education and experience have never allowed
them to see children with disabilities and the way they learn. They
expected to visit special schools as part of the in-service course but
unfortunately, such an activity was not included in the course
programme. The course brought together teachers from both special and
mainstream schools and it was expected that during the course the
participants would exchange experiences. However, teachers emphasise
that talking and discussing is not enough and they need to see special
schools with their own eyes.

It is felt that a great advantage for a teacher in terms of adopting a critical approach to segregation is the experience of both types – mainstream and special schools. There are only two teachers who have taught in both types of school among those interviewed, but they express the opinions of professionals who are more broad-minded than their colleagues who have worked only in one type of school.

> *When I came from a mainstream school to teach in a special school, it was difficult for me work with children who were so different from the students I was used to. I had to feel my way through using my intuition. There was a boy who was diagnosed as ineducable. Now, I can analyse that to help him I used a one-to-one approach and can say now what was wrong with him. When he was 3 his mother abandoned him, when he was 6 the teacher decided that he should repeat the year. As a result, his self- esteem fell so low that he could not study. I am glad and proud that now he is again in a mainstream school and that I felt at the right time that there had been a mistake.*

Resources

Lack of resources stands out as the problem that is constantly referred to by teachers and headteachers. The thoughts are expressed in the very emotional tone of people who are very tired or disappointed:

> *I've got three vacancies for teachers in the school and cannot find anybody. Nobody wants to get involved in such difficult work for such a miserable salary.*

> *In our state, no matter how hard teachers try, the children are not guaranteed any secure future.*

The course participants constantly compare what they have seen in other countries with the situation in Russia. They confidently assert that resources are the main reason for success in integration abroad:

> *We cannot even compare them and us. They have everything.*

> *And integration, of course, they can afford it. Any need of a child is met. There are laboratories that work to meet the needs of all children. If a child needs an individual chair, he is provided with one. In our schools, these children will die because of the conditions.*

> *Of course, another thing that struck us – resources. They do not have to spend nights writing cards for the lesson. We*

*simply realised how much time we waste. We could simply use
a computer.*

The Teacher Retraining Course – a new approach

Assessment of the course by the participants. The course is assessed very highly by all participants. The assessment can be classified into two categories – personal and professional. The personal aspect of the assessment is very important. It has been mentioned in several interviews that in Russia, retraining courses are very often regarded as an obligatory part of teachers' work and teachers are assigned to undertake some course irrespective of their wish. This accounts for a frequent usage of the verb 'to be sent' to a course instead of 'go' or 'choose to go'.

The interviews indicate that the in-service course that is offered at the Perm State Pedagogical University attracts professionals who are very interested in their work and consider their profession an integral part of their life.

*I had such a difficult time in my life. I was in need of a
change. Then I heard about the course and as a teacher with a
lot of experience, I got immediately interested in it.*

*Normally, such courses in our system are very formal. The
administration sends you and you have to attend. But this
time I did not have such a feeling. I knew why I was attending
the course. The atmosphere was encouraging, pleasant.*

One of the main reasons given to explain this is that the course starts with psychological training. Teachers consider it very helpful both personally and professionally. All the participants agree that the training has helped them in learning how to understand themselves and overcome the problems that arise from psychological illiteracy, which they define as the lack of knowledge about oneself.

*Teachers were reserved themselves and had their own
complexes. How can a teacher who has her own problems and
cannot formulate them deal with problems of children? The
training made a big difference. Teachers started asking
questions: 'How has it happened? How shall I overcome this
problem?'*

*We became very friendly. And I looked forward to coming to
these sessions though they were very intense. Very warm,
friendly attitude to everybody. Everybody feels that they are
wanted and accepted. People who had got to the course by
accident left after the second or third class.*

Whole School Approach as Developed within the Retraining Course

'Whole school' aspects of the course. The issue of prime interest in this area is whether the project aimed to reach the level where all the professionals will operate within a whole school approach. A whole school approach can be interpreted in different ways; however, the interpretation given by Mittler (1992) and Simmons (1986) is seen as most appropriate for this study, as it provides the basic points for defining a 'whole school approach'. They have identified three main areas of competence for teachers to acquire during a retraining course. One of the ways to analyse the project's contribution to a whole school approach is to see how far these points have been realised:

1. awareness of students' needs;
2. responsibility for using appropriate techniques;
3. access to specialised help.

1. Awareness of students' needs. The information that the participants received during the course served as a revelation. The majority of participants who had never worked in a special school did not know before the course what sort of children they worked with. Some special school teachers admit that they had no special education before the course and experienced considerable difficulties in their work. All participants expressed appreciation of such courses as psychology, neuro-psychology and corrective pedagogy. They acknowledge that these courses threw light upon the nature of the children they worked with.

> *By the time I started at my school, I had never seen so many disabled children. I had always worked with healthy, intelligent children and I came to work in a special school because of a higher salary. And when we were studying the brain and which function each part of the brain was performing, I became aware of why some children behaved in this or that way. Now when a child is shouting or crying I can identify why it is happening. The child may be epileptic or something.*

A mainstream schoolteacher acknowledges that these specialist elements of the course helped her in developing a programme she uses in a corrective class. Importantly, she feels she works now at a higher professional level:

> *When developing the programme I used the knowledge I received on our psychology, neuro-psychology and play therapy courses. The play therapy helps to develop memory, attention and so on.*

An advantage for the four interviewees who went on study visits either to the Netherlands or England was an opportunity to observe teachers from other countries at work and acquire new techniques to be used in their practice. All four participants appreciate the new knowledge they acquired but show a high degree of selectivity in deciding what can and cannot be used in their context of Russian schools:

> I have brought back lots of elements of management activity that I have observed in Oxford schools.

> Even the way the school looks reflects some of the elements that we have adopted. There are photos on the doors but there are also lots of elements behind the doors which are not seen but they are there.

> We were also interested in the system of education. But we cannot change ours. We can take only some elements from their system but there are constraints even for this.

2. *Responsibility for using appropriate techniques.* In terms of responsibility for using appropriate techniques, all the teachers and school managers state they are quite confident in the techniques they are using. They do not indicate that they lack techniques. The area indicated as problematic is lack of knowledge of differentiation. In this respect, the international sessions and seminars have been most helpful. The participants recognise this:

> The British lecturers concentrated mostly on how they use an individual approach in their classes. I admire the way they see an individual need of a particular child. They know when it is necessary to come up to the child and pat him on the shoulder, for example. And what is most important they can explain why they are doing it.

> Our teachers (who receive such a low salary) are simply enthusiasts, people who use all their soul in their work. They have certainly collected all the materials they needed and will be able, believe me, to interpret them and apply them creatively in their work.

The four interviewees who did not go on study visits express a wish to learn more about practices abroad. Unfortunately, there is no indication that they have managed to learn a lot from the participants who have been abroad. They all emphasise that one can learn only from seeing everything with one's own eyes.

3. *Access to specialised help.* Almost all participants refer to not having a 'teaching assistant'. A teaching assistant as a notion is a novelty for Russian teachers. They mention the problem only because they have had a chance to learn about it from their foreign colleagues. They all realise

that having extra help in the classroom is essential but prevented by the lack of financial resources. One of the teachers says:

Of course, it is easier for them to work as they have more adults in the classroom. Where shall we take money for it?

Change Agents

The idea of an in-service teacher retraining course preparing 'change agents' was promoted throughout the life of the project, and the research has helped in identifying whether the participants have managed to become leaders of inclusion activity in schools or not. According to some of the interviewees, the idea of preparing individuals who would become the centre of activity in the area of SEN permeates the course. However, the answer to the question of whether course participants became real change agents is not straightforward.

The opinion of participants on what has been achieved and what they understand by achievement differs immensely from individual to individual. Some participants emphasise personal changes and changes in their classrooms, while others realise that change is required at a whole school level. Several examples have become 'celebrities' within the project. The activities developed by these teachers have become so well known because these are changes at a formal level, and it is obvious from the interviews that teachers and principals consider such changes to be genuine. It is the scope of changes that is seen as crucial.

Lena has written a programme and works in accordance with it. She constantly makes presentations at pedagogical meetings and teachers like what she is talking about.

Thus, a 'programme' is considered to be a bigger shift than informal consultations in a deputy head's office or in an ordinary conversation. One participant, a special school deputy, describes her consultations, which she gives if a young teacher is at a loss:

In terms of 'corrective work', I can give some sound advice to the teachers at school. If a teacher comes to me and explains what difficulties the child experiences I can trace the reasons and she cannot do this.

Another participant declares that there have not been any changes or shifts in the work of teachers. She expresses bitter thoughts:

Lena and our tutors try writing a plan for integration. All others work as they used to.

At the same time, this teacher regrets that she cannot use the knowledge of psychology gained during the course. Her argument is that teachers are not allowed to offer psychological help because they may be accused of non-professionalism:

> *We are not allowed to provide psychological help though we know how to do it.*

Thus, the statement 'there are no changes' is compounded with contradictions when teachers describe their intentions for future development or their everyday practice at school. There is development at an individual professional level, but teachers find it difficult to organise other teachers and unite their efforts in work with SEN. There are several reasons for this. First, teachers feel isolated from each other. They believe that the number of professionals who have the same knowledge and, more important, the same understanding of special education and inclusion issues is small:

> *One of the problems is that there are not many like-minded people. Not many of us have taken the course. And to implement something new we have to try it, to touch it, to feel it. We cannot do it in a different way.*

There is another kind of isolation that almost all participants have mentioned. They complain that other professionals are eager to learn and take ideas, materials, etc. from them but they do not give anything in return:

> *We want to share, but other teachers from other schools want to take without wishing to give anything back. Other teachers say: prepare, give it to us. No. We want a mutual, creative activity.*

Another reason for the lack of organised change activity in the SEN area is administrative control, or lack of it. This stands out as one of the most important factors and teachers draw comparisons between 'good' and 'bad' administrators. The 'celebrity' cases referred to earlier are considered to have been successful owing to strong support that the teacher gets from the school administration.

The headteacher at Lena's school is very proud of her. She mentions her everywhere and gives her a free hand wherever possible.

> *[Question: What are the changes in your work?]*
> *Well, changes do not depend on me but on how the administration looks at it.*

The fact that administration occupies such a strong position has not been ignored by the initiators of the course. They realise the importance of headteacher awareness of the ideas that teachers encounter on the retraining course. One tutor who was directly involved in the training of school managers explains this:

> *Special courses were arranged for school managers. That is,*
> *the content of the teacher training course was incorporated*
> *into the managers' training programme. As a result, the school*
> *heads who had realised the importance of the work with SEN*
> *supported the teachers in conducting their projects.*

Permeation

Preparing teachers to work with SEN within the retraining course is described by Mittler (1992) as part of the permeation approach which helps to provide all teachers with an opportunity to learn about SEN. The activities of the TEMPUS-TACIS project were not confined to developing the retraining course. Additional activities that were considered integral included courses for managers and an undergraduate course within the department of pre-school education. This course was devised to prepare social pedagogues and the project assisted in obtaining a licence. In addition, the University has established a course on issues of special education that is obligatory for all students.

It was to the advantage of the project that there was awareness of the importance of permeation at an organisational level. The idea of introducing an SEN element has been promoted from the beginning of the project. Teachers also realise that preparation should start early but emphasise the importance of retraining of teachers. In their opinion, only experienced teachers know what is required in the classroom and therefore they can make a more effective use of the information.

> *I wish the programme had embraced more teachers. It is good*
> *that students get training at universities but it is different with*
> *teachers who have experience. I know exactly what I need and*
> *a student may gain knowledge without knowing where she will*
> *apply it.*

The TEMPUS-TACIS Development as an International Project

Trans-European context. All interviewees were asked whether the development in Perm and the University would have been possible if the project were not international. The answers are of two kinds – some believe that it would not have been possible but would have taken much more time and would have developed on too big a scale:

> *We would have been boiling in our own juice. The exchanges*
> *would have been among different schools or maybe cities. But*
> *we are all Russians with practically the same thinking. Their*
> *thinking is quite different. That is why the outcomes have*

> *appeared to be more productive than if we had been doing it*
> *on our own.*

Others think that no developments would have been possible without the project. They emphasise the role of the project as an initiator of a new notion that was first introduced in the Perm educational community.

> *The project has given a scientific ground to the vague notions*
> *we had before. It has given a push for all the activities.*
> *Teachers had been on their own. Attention at last was drawn*
> *to the problems they faced in their work.*

Political role of the project. Another important aspect of the project was its effect on policy-making and administration. Its exclusive role in this respect is clearly described by one of the coordinators:

> *[Question: Would it have been possible to achieve what has*
> *been achieved if the project were not international?]*
> *Generally speaking, yes, but not that quickly. This project,*
> *through our 'subtle' use of it, has served as a catalyst. You*
> *understand very well the way our administrators work.*
> *Administration has always got money for a bright event, but*
> *not for everyday activities. The Pedagogical University with all*
> *these ideas would have met understanding from them but all*
> *action would have been postponed for several years. But when*
> *administrators heard that three respectable universities try to*
> *work with us, they immediately got motivated to act quicker*
> *and better than they normally do. And I respect those people*
> *who worked with us all these years – they are the celebrities of*
> *the project.*

The Russian managers have been directing the project in this way, taking advantage of the fact that Russian administration still looks at Western countries with awe and is always ready to demonstrate the best of their skills. For the British coordinator, this achievement is among the unintended outcomes of the project:

> *I also accept that an international project can be used in a*
> *political and tactical way. Fine, I do not worry about it in the*
> *slightest.*

It should be emphasised that in a different context the project would not have become such a driving force for new developments. It is through skilful manipulation of a typically Russian phenomenon and through acceptance of this method by the members of the team that the change has taken place.

Teamwork and personal agendas. Almost all the participants attribute the great success of the project to the ethos that permeated the project throughout its duration. The project is characterised as 'excellent', 'wonderful' and 'unforgettable'. It is evident that the memories of the project involve many emotions.

> *There is a certain ideological problem that has been solved for me. I have learnt that in Europe people are like any other people. These people achieve great results in their work. Their humanism and democracy have risen to extremely high levels. We have a long way to go. But experience of their work indicates that we will arrive at the same results because they have not achieved theirs in one day.*

The British coordinator defines this phenomenon as 'personal agendas' – new communication has been conducive to enlarging horizons and consciousness:

> *Any new relationship with any new group of people – you are learning about yourself in relationship with others. So, yes, I learnt a lot from other people and am very fond of the people I have met. That is, I think, as important as subject matter.*
>
> *In all of these aspects, there is an important social relationship which is not just a matter of academic tourism but really finding out more about each other.*

The project has gained from the fact that almost every participant was interested in SEN but pursued their own agenda to realise particular individual aims. Some team members contributed to the initial and final research for the project in Perm. In addition, the project has given them a rare chance to conduct their own research and continue their PhD work. Several young members of the team have received an opportunity to continue their studies in the universities of Amsterdam and Oxford. What is important is that personal agendas have merged into one common agenda of the project.

Practical implications. Overall, the project has been a significant success and the participants realise that. However, some of them, and especially headteachers, are aware of elements that can be improved. The main points of concern are the need for better communication and information exchange among different members of the project; and more appropriate use of the resource centre.

The teachers and headteachers have pointed out that though they met many participants of the project, they are not completely sure what each of them was doing and what was each individual contribution to the project. They also admit that they would have liked to learn more from each other. An important factor identified by them is a better reporting system among all the members:

*I have kept a diary during all the study visits in Oxford and
Germany and I was ready to report about everything. That is
what I did when I came home to Perm. But, unfortunately, I
have no idea what other members saw in Amsterdam, for
example. I have not seen a single report even if there were one.
I think that there must be a better link among all those who
participate in the project.*

An issue that almost all teachers and headteachers expanded on is the
usage of the resource centre, which has been established to provide
teachers with further support. It is fully equipped and this year a
psychology consultancy service will be offered there for parents to get
help from an independent consultant concerning the diagnosis of their
child. However, teachers emphasise that they expected more from this
centre. They need the centre to provide them with the translation
material that the project has provided and complain that it does not work
very quickly. They want the centre to act as a coordinating body for them
to meet and exchange their new developments:

*The centre is there to collect materials. Nobody has asked for
any materials from schools. It would be nice to look through
some dissertations of other course participants. Somebody
from the first group has written something on my topic but I
could not find anything there in the centre. The computer and
printer alone are not yet a centre. We could not find any
diplomas.*

*We want to come and meet again and we thought that the
centre could help us with this. But it does not happen.*

Conclusion

The project addressed the important issue of a humanistic approach to
educating disabled children. An international perspective demonstrates
that developing inclusive practices is not an exclusively Russian
problem. Other more developed countries have experienced similar
problems. It is accepted that during the transitional period from a
specialised approach to inclusive education, emphasis should be placed
on retraining teachers (Ainscow & Floreck, 1988). Teachers continue
their work at schools as change agents (Diniz, 1991), trying to
disseminate inclusive ideas and good practice in working with special
needs children. Teacher retraining courses are expected to develop
appropriate values and qualities in teachers and promote a whole school
approach. This means that teachers should work as a team and in
collaboration with other specialists in the area.

Despite certain organisational problems, the project has fulfilled its main purpose. The outcomes of the project are sustainable without the project's intervention. The course goes on and the participants perceive it as like any other retraining course and do not associate it with the project. This has been identified as the main target for other similar projects. The idea that the participants of the TEMPUS-TACIS project have learnt from practice is to invest in the future and go beyond the limits of the project's influence.

References

Ainscow, M. & Florek, A. (Eds) (1989) *Special Educational Needs: towards a whole school approach.* London: David Fulton.

Bîrzea, C. (1996) Education in a World of Transition: between post-communism and post-modernism, *Prospects,* 26, pp. 673-682.

Diniz, F.A. (1991) Special Education: an overview of recent changes, European *Journal of Special Needs Education,* 14(2), pp. 15-30.

Goneev, A. (1999) *Osnovi Korrektsionnoy Pedagogiki.* Moscow: Academia.

Goutnick, G. (1999) *Development of Special Education in Perm for 1995-2000.* Perm: Department of Education.

Lutovinov, V. & Poletaev, E. (1998) Ideologia Vospitania Rossiyskoy Molodezshi, *Pedagogika,* No. 5, pp. 46-51.

Mittler, P. (1992) Preparing All Initial Teacher Training Students to Teach Children with Special Educational Needs: a case study from England, *European Journal of Special Needs Education,* 7(1), pp. 1-10.

Simmons, K. (1986) Painful Extractions, *Times Educational Supplement,* 17 October.

Van der Wolf, K. & Sayer, J. (1999) *Opening Schools for All.* Leuven-Apeldoorn: Garant.

Vygotsky (1986) *Thought and Language.* Cambridge MA: MIT Press.

The Process of Transition: teacher biographies and teachers' actions

HARTMUT WENZEL & GUDRUN MEISTER

Introduction

The political and economic changes of 1989/90, which marked the end of the German Democratic Republic (GDR) and the entry of the five newly formed East German *Länder* into the legal and social system of the German Federal Republic, are the historical connecting points for a project which we are reporting here. These changes, which are named, for short, the '*Wende*', or turning point, are themselves part of a much wider process of transformation which relates to the collapse of the former Soviet Union and its ideological foundations; to changes in social patterns and values in a context of more general processes of modernisation, and in part to global changes and competitive processes resulting from scientific and technical developments.

In some senses, the political, economic and social collapses and changes or processes of transition in the new German Länder are examples for processes of transformation taking place in other central and east European states, from the Soviet Union as a centralised power, in the transition from a one-party system to a pluralistic democracy, or from a centrally planned economy to a capitalist market economy (Pachocinski, 1996). These usually result in a multiplicity of drastic changes, whether at state economic level or at the level of social institutions and associations, or not least on the level of subjective experience and behaviour. Such processes of transformation are not linear progressive modernisation or successive accommodation of one system to an apparently superior one. Rather, they proceed in contradictory, unsynchronised complex ambiguities, and moreover, with discontinuities and reformulations of interactive state, social and individual levels. They also touch the level of meanings and perspectives and aims and essential foundations of education and pedagogical practice within the new frameworks.

In this chapter, we are reporting on our research project because we are persuaded that the problems of educational restructuring which we have encountered and continue to untangle in the new German Länder may contribute to understanding of developments in other countries, and in particular, for school development processes within our shared TEMPUS project in Perm.

After the 1989/90 Wende, a process began of rapid and complex social changes, which also included the restructuring of education. Because of the changes in political ideology and of the unification treaty's resolved alignments with West German regulations, there were considerable changes in almost all aspects related to schools (laws, structures, regulations etc.) After the introduction of the new school structures, it was possible to conclude from the many views expressed by teachers that, despite overall agreement with a number of school changes (especially the removal of ideology), and after an initial phase of reformist euphoria, they experienced the drastic process of change to the school system after the Wende not just as desirable democratic renewal but often as top-down, steered by the new holders of political power. Many felt excluded from participation in this phase, with massive loss of confidence, job insecurity, and continually on the receiving end of what were felt to be authoritarian dictates of the legislature and education administrators (Harms, 1992).

So, we were faced with a paradox in the context of the Wende – as identified by Händle et al (1998) – that a publicly discredited teaching body extensively criticised for its attitudes and competence levels had with scant preparation to take on the responsibility in practice for the restructuring of schooling. After the Wende, it was unclear how far the political and economic discontinuity and the subsequent processes of school reform were to prompt critical reflection on pedagogical practice and possible change, since both before and after the Wende there remained sufficient scope for self-determination, initiative and redefinition, but also for rejection, withdrawal and protecting one's corner.

Looked at from outside, it is possible to assume that many teachers in the new Länder had to review their pedagogical positions and practice and their career perspectives. The attitude was deeply ingrained that teachers were a key pillar of GDR society and its political ideology. However, that has to be distinguished from the personal perspectives of teachers. Thus, it is clear from studies by Döbert (1997) that even before the Wende, various individual critiques were made of political and ideological demands and expectations on teaching. Teachers could hardly escape from specific political requirements, but there were areas of scope for shaping pedagogical practice, and these were used. From the personal perspective of teachers, the Wende was experienced not just as the immediate collapse of everyone's previous world, but as a potential liberation from political ballast and disliked children's reins. In such cases, there would be no compulsion to fundamental reflection on one's personal role as a teacher in the GDR schools system; indeed, any such requirement would be seen as unjustified. Generally, it was a relief to be able to cast off the political ballast and focus more clearly on the transmission of one's specialist subjects in accordance with a professional ethic and the perceived interests of children. Emphasis on one's teaching subject meant relief from burdens; it promised security in the face of hostility, and legitimate continuity of classroom practice.

There were and still are overt and covert forms of continuity. That is particularly true of everyday classroom practice. The frequently emphasised total change in schooling after the Wende becomes, on closer scrutiny, much less spectacular than expected. A substantial foundation of the school system remained: state organisation and its related structures of responsibility and supervision. School transformation proceeded in a relatively stable framework, retaining, in terms of organisational theory, a significant structural foundation in the common history and tradition of both Germanys (Zymek, 1992, 1996).

From this background, here but briefly sketched, derived the idea for our project. Our enquiry aimed to discover how those teachers already in service in GDR times dealt with the Wende and, in that context, with the transition to a new school system with changed ideological foundations; what were the effects of the Wende on their concepts, or more specifically, on their models of interpretation and action; and what, in the new circumstances, has been their readiness to participate in school development? The development of schools, according to recent research on school quality, school comparisons and school development, depends, along with leadership, above all, on teachers. It is they, through their day-to-day pedagogical practice in schools, who bring institutional policies to life. On them, individually and collegiately, largely depend what aims are pursued, what rules are followed, what results are achieved, how emergent problems and conflicts are treated, and how innovation and new thinking are absorbed into the daily life of the school.

This complexity of issues [1] prompts us, on the one hand, to seek access to teachers' current conceptual patterns for practice, and on the other, to study what has happened to teachers' career biographies with these current patterns of thought. Accordingly, we conceived of our project principally as a union of two methodological approaches: we used the teachers' observations when confronted with their own video-recorded lessons, together with descriptive career biography interviews.

In video confrontations [2], the video-recorded lesson is played back to the sample of teachers as a 'stimulated recall technique' in order to reflect back on their own teaching, and the observations prompted by this process are recorded for later analysis. Clearly, this brings up, above all, those subjective theories and patterns of thought which are connected with concrete practice. To grasp, or at least begin to gauge the genesis of such thought patterns, but at the same time also to trace back the development of career biographies and the personal experience and assimilation of the Wende, we conducted career biography interviews with the sample of teachers [3], before using the lesson recordings.

So, the subject matter of our investigations was lesson-related subjective structures of meaning, and their genesis and development in the particular circumstances of social and political change and the school reforms connected with it. We investigated in particular whether and how far teachers' own understandings of their practice and roles underwent change associated with the Wende.

What follows is an example of our procedure, followed by a discussion of some outcomes. We conclude with reflections on outcomes of this approach, with particular attention to those aspects which may be relevant to the TEMPUS project.

Case Study: Mr Thalstett

Outline Biography of Mr Thalstett

Childhood and youth: the painful road to self-discovery. Born early in the 1960s, Mr Thalstett, now a *gymnasium* [4] teacher, had, with repeated removals and changes of school, a somewhat untypical childhood for the GDR. His parents divorced when he was 8. Living through their separation remains as a deeply painful experience, but the experiences which stand out as especially significant determinants for later life are profound identity crises together with being marginalised, as a result of losing intimate relationships (his mother moves to her new husband in another *Land*), and the problematic experiences in the new family constellation. Mr Thalstett was not accepted by his new stepfather for his own sake, but had to struggle for recognition (and also the transfer of family name and adoption) by outstanding achievements. The lack of security or acceptance were not adequately compensated by his mother, who was often kept away from home by her intensive involvements in the Party. Against this background of problematic family experiences, long stretches of his biography read as a quest for social relationships and personal identity.

In this situation, school assumed a most significant biographical importance. The school's Pioneer and State Youth Organisation compensated in some senses for the lack of family warmth. Mr Thalstett clearly identifies that, because of the family situation, extracurricular activities of child and youth organisations assumed considerable socialising importance – the pedagogical is interwoven here with the political; extracurricular activities developed through social bonding and strong political socialisation with a high sense of identity.

Very good school grades – despite changes of school there were few problems in achieving high marks – took him up from year 9 to the pre-university EOS [5]. This was the time when he at last was given the new family name.

Choice of career: coming round to a career in teaching. Mr Thalstett's path towards teaching is closely linked to his self-discovery and emancipation. He tried out a variety of different areas of activity and finally went his own way. His decision to teach emerged only after his specialised training was concluded and his wish to work in a children's home proved not to be possible.

Teaching was the alternative route for working with children and at least in some degree to be able to assume a father figure role. From his literary interests came the decision to combine the subjects of German and Russian. An important experience was the year of study in the Soviet Union just at the start of the Gorbachov era. The seminar group formed there, where he also met his future wife, was able to take a large measure of responsibility for shaping the form and content of study: 'That's where I experienced how people blossomed'. In this mood of radical change, the work of the Party group there opened up to him, and in spring 1987, under the combined influence of glasnost and perestroika, Mr Thalstett joined the SED [6]. But on returning to the GDR, he was bitterly disappointed by the Party gatherings at university and Party meetings in his practice school.

The Wende: torn between scepticism and change. In August 1989, after passing his final examinations with very high marks, he started in his teaching post. It was at this time that the first demonstrations and streams of refugees were starting; the collapse of the Communist state was by now inevitable. At this point, he and his wife, also a teacher, could not really identify with the protests. Interestingly, he describes the Wende as 'a private matter', identifying the situation in which teachers in the school hardly discussed political developments, even though the effects (classmates going West with their parents, access to independent television, etc.) were, of course, in evidence there.

In this process, to which he ascribes a period of over 2 years, phases of hope succeeded to phases of disenchantment. Consciously using the new found freedom, he left the Party when he came to doubt its capacity to reform. For a time after the Wende, teaching continued at his 'polytechnical school' and Mr Thalstett was able to invest his views of the teaching role in helping the children of his year 5 class as far as possible to come to terms with the confusions of the Wende. Whilst the Wende itself created a number of new problems (for example, his wife lost her job and with their new baby they had to pay the rent for a flat at 'new German' prices), these paled into insignificance for him, in comparison with the effects of the subsequent school reforms.

Because Russian lost its status as a subject (English becoming almost everywhere the first foreign language), he was personally under threat because the subject basis for a secure teaching career had gone. All the greater was his relief when he applied for and was moved to the Caroline Gymnasium. So, contrary to fears, the structural school reform opened up new possibilities for Mr Thalstett, even though he was somewhat sceptical about the gymnasium, which was formed from a former elite polytechnic school. This scepticism also derived from uncertainty whether he would be in a position to meet the, as yet, unclear expectations of the gymnasium. Certainly, he was aware that coming into the new school situation with his subject combination of German and Russian, he was entering a problem area.

Through in-service study of a new subject (social studies) he made his new position in the gymnasium secure, and later began a new in-service training course for the subject of ethics, still to be completed by the time of our interview.

View of being a teacher. Before Mr Thalstett came to the gymnasium, he had got to know other schools, as a pupil (POS [7], EOS) and later as a student (POS) and newly qualified teacher (POS). However, as a pupil or student, his experience of school was without the perspective of a future teacher, since this career choice came later. But school acquired especial importance for him as a familiar situation in which he experienced problems. In the career/biographical interview, he continually refers to this, with the emphasis not so much on lessons, content and method. With these, he had no problems worth mentioning, either as a pupil or later in teaching practice or the early years of teaching. To that extent, one can surmise that he more or less consciously followed well-tried traditions. It is much more the class group and extracurricular activities of his own schooldays which are important for him, for these gave him stable self-esteem and promoted self-consciousness. His picture of 'the good school' is clearly influenced by these experiences. Mr Thalstett emphasises 'pastoral pedagogy'. In a 'good school', this has to be 'up and running'. He sees himself less as a teacher and more as a pastoral figure. A good teacher must create free activity space for pupils. Pedagogy consists, above all, of the extracurricular activities, which the teacher creates with his form-group.

This understanding grew from his own school experience as a pupil and was confirmed in his time at the POS. In those days, extracurricular activities were to a large extent built in as a programme strongly motivated by political collective education. In the context of school reform, there was an end to both the previous duty on teachers to share activities with their class groups and also the financial and organisational foundations for them. Mr Thalstett had painful experience of this process in the transfer from his previous POS to the Carolineum, and on top of this came the greater emphasis on academic results in the new school structure of the gymnasium.

Understanding of classroom teaching: pupil-centred or institutionally constrained. Mr Thalstett regretfully identifies the effects of pressure for good marks and achievement in his new school; he can see the need to adapt to other ways of working in the classroom, but does not yet carry them out. In striving for social acceptance, Mr Thalstett feels a contradiction between the demands on him as a human being, on the one hand, and on the other hand, as a teacher. He takes the view that the priority being given to achievement represents in general a worsening of the school situation, but has no real conception of an alternative. It is here that a dilemma embedded in his biography becomes clear. His basic view of 'social pedagogy' is in conflict with the school system of marks and achievement. Institutional constraints contradict his wishes to foster relationships. The institutional focus on achievement and discipline emerges as the antithesis of his human purposes.

To summarise: it is clearly established in this case that the social and political Wende of 19889/90 was a happening for which he had not actively striven, so had to put up with. It led to pressure to change and accommodate in many spheres of everyday living, with many uncertainties and disappointments, but also hopes. The radical changes involved in the process of social and political transformation did not become clear immediately, but over time. For Mr Thalstett, the process of transfer to a new school structure with new guidelines, regulations etc. was the event which in its concrete effects was more significant than the transition to the legal and social system of the Federal Republic.

This problematic personal understanding of the roles of teaching and the teacher were derived from analysis of the career biographical interview. Given the method adopted, we can now check how far such problems in fact emerge in the classroom, how they are picked up and commented upon, and perhaps what patterns of thinking and understanding inform them.

Mr Thalstett's Classroom Teaching

The first commentary in the video playback, which is later analysed more closely, relates to the following scene before the German lesson in year 10 of a gymnasium. It is period 4, which is from 10.25 to 11.10.

The 'Kathi scene'

Teacher: Well, Miss Heinze.
Pupil: Doesn't make sense.

> *T: What?*
> *P: What's going to be in the next test?*
> *T: Everything.*
> *P: What do you mean, everything?*
> *T: Everything.*
> *P: From ...*
> *T: Everything.*
> *P: Do you know how much that is?*
> *T: Yes.*
> *P: You realise it's at least 25 pages?*
> *T: Too bad.*
> *P: And we're supposed to learn all that?*
> *T: Yes.*
> *P: By heart? ... That's great!*
> *T: Kathi, I'll narrow that down again tomorrow.*
> *P: Not till tomorrow?*
> *T: Not till tomorrow.*
> *P: How many hours are we writing?*
> *T: One hour.*
> *P. Only one hour?*
> *T: Add a note it can't be that much with only one hour to write. You'll be writing for one hour under supervision.*

Analysis of the video-recording from an observer viewpoint leads to the following evaluation. When the teacher enters the classroom, pupils register the fact, at most, marginally. The teacher busies himself unpacking and arranging his lesson materials. A degree of agitation and haste can be seen from his movements and repeated talking to himself. His actions appear incoherent. He frequently checks, interrupts his preparations and rearranges his materials. He sometimes realises he is turning away from the class; he stops sorting, appears less rushed and hasty, and turns to the class with a smile.

That is the situation in which a girl comes up to him with the question about the next piece of class homework. At first, the teacher glances at her with a smile, but then brushes aside her request dismissively. After a further attempt by the girl to ask the teacher about the amount of the work which might be tested, the teacher finally puts the girl down. After a brief pause, he turns to the girl, now sitting in her place, and announces that in the German lesson on the following day, he will once again set a limit to the contents expected in the homework.

Analysis of the Video Playback

When Mr Thalstett begins his comments, he selects the scene described above. Although this scene is somewhat marginal in character, it seems so significant to Mr Thalstett that he enlarges on it. He describes the scene as a frequently occurring minor power game which pupils cannot resist. Mr Thalstett stands for a broad cultural understanding which presupposes all-embracing interest. Kathi's question, by contrast, represents a calculated pupil attitude, of wanting to learn only what is going to count for marks. So, the teacher's symbolic demonstration of power in this power game represents a rejection and distancing from pupils' insistence on utilitarian reduction and selective learning. But, on the personal level, there are undesired side effects which break with Mr Thalstett's basic commitment to good relationships with pupils. In the sequel, he brings out repair strategies, to restore the previously strained relationship with the pupils. He expresses understanding for the pupils' wishes and gives way to the tactic deployed by Kathi. It is important for him to clear up the situation so that his relationships are not damaged. His basic commitment to being close to pupils, even when that constitutes a breach of institutional contexts, emerges as the pattern in this teacher's behaviour.

At the start of the lesson, Mr Thalstett then refers to the homework, in order to avoid negative feelings affecting communications in this lesson. However, he still makes it clear in his commentary that he does not associate himself with the pupils' tactics. That means Mr Thalstett is in a vicious circle: through his empathy with pupils and/or fear of losing relationships, he is in reality subject to an institutional role definition which emphasises the function of selection. Through pupil-centredness, he comes to a shift of aims, from a broad educational mission to narrow thinking about achievement, looking for quantifiable content. An implicit dilemma is apparent from the starting exchanges, and comes out clearly later: pupils' lack of interest in wider aspects of the subject is attributable not only to their calculating underlying attitude, but Mr. Thalstett is unable to motivate them to work on the content of the lesson. The lesson follows exclusively teacher-centred whole class patterns.

Summarising Remarks on the Thalstett Case Study

The constellation of problems formulated in the concluding remarks from the biographical interview has become more specific in the extracted scenes and commentary. In his teaching, Mr Thalstett faces a dilemma to which he currently has no solution. He has an understanding of education adequate for gymnasium teaching and more broadly based, which, if possible, he would wish to develop in intensive and relevant work with pupils. That is why – especially with his biographical background – good relationships with his pupils are important to him. But pupils' interests are determined by the demands of the institution, i.e. they want through calculated effort to come out well in situations which test achievement. Mr Thalstett, by going along with the needs signalled by his pupils, is at the same time betraying his own educational intentions. His attitude of high expectations for pupils is damaged by the general structure geared to selection. He recognises and empathises with pupils' interests, which are determined by the school culture, accedes to these, and so he too perpetuates an approach to teaching targeted at verifiable knowledge. As the lesson sketch shows, he has developed no adequate teaching competencies to cope with his very real dilemma in this situation, so he reverts to traditional front-of-class teaching methods.

Whilst his reference to more open teaching methods points to a direction in which to develop, he is in danger of being trapped in traditional patterns because of the narrow and immediate interests of pupils. This situation, which he indicates is unsatisfying, also leads to inadequate strategies for teacher-pupil relationships. He works off his own frustration and disillusionment through irony and power games. Paradoxically, this reinforces the selection structure which he dislikes. The results are feelings of alienation and distance.

Mr Thalstett reached his political and private positions in the new republic about 6 years after the Wende. His horizons of norms and values were markedly modified but in some fundamental aspects remain unchanged. In relation to the new professional situation, we can establish that Mr Thalstett accommodates increasingly and comes to terms with the new gymnasium school structure and what he perceives to be its demands for such high levels of achievement. But one dilemma emerging from his biography remains acute. His basic attitude of social pedagogy is in conflict with the school's system of high marks and discipline, which has even greater importance in an elite gymnasium. He feels a burdensome contradiction between his wishes for good relationships with pupils and also with colleagues, and the institutional constraints, which he may criticise sharply but for which he has developed no strategies to lessen the problem.

Some Conclusions

In our project, we deliberately concentrated on teachers' individual personality, experience and coming to terms with the Wende, and paid particular attention to their view of classroom teaching activity (the internal perspective).

Whereas immediately after the Wende it was rather the disruptions and hiatuses from the external perspective which were identified, another picture emerges from the career biographical inner perspective – at least for those teachers who continued to teach in schools after the Wende. For them personally, the dismantling of the Berlin Wall or the end of the GDR was of course significant and important, but that is not the predominant intrusion in their own life-paths or the particular critical event in their career. Much more problematical and, as it were, existentially threatening, was the experience of transition into the new school structures (Fuhrmann, 1996). In this situation, problems are suddenly bundled together which are unusual in this phase of a teacher's personal or professional career (see Hubermann, 1989):

competitive application for appointment to a form of school in a changed school system unknown from personal experience and without specific training;

dependency on decision-making committees, whose criteria for deciding on placement in one or other of the new types of school are not always known and transparent;

the experience of a threat to professional existence caused by subjects becoming redundant or in less demand;

closure of existing schools and the social networks connected to them (school staff body and work context);

introduction to a new or at least changed school staff, usually also with a new head);

change of composition of pupils, both for the previous POS teachers now teaching in secondary schools without the top third of the ability range, and for the previous EOS teachers now teaching in the gymnasium, beginning at age 12;

new regulations and also, in many instances, new text books;

changes in the social status of teachers;

changes in the coverage and priority given to individual teaching subjects;

possible loss of functions in the previous school system, or taking on new functions.

When looking at the events of the Wende from the internal perspective of teachers, it becomes clear that the Wende is part of the whole biographical process, which comprises, as well as the professional part, other aspects such as family, relatives and friends, residential context etc., which normally run in quite different kinds of rhythms and whose structures therefore bring different kinds of continuity, or at least are not greatly influenced by the introduction of new school structures (Krause & Wenzel, 1998).

Because of the temporal and institutional framework of requirements, the teaching body depended on continuing its activity on the foundations of its previous professional competencies, both for the establishment of order and for the enablement of basic functions of schools' interaction. If teachers did not want to give up their professional existence, they were required to apply competitively and justify themselves by their professional activity. It made sense for them to revert to elementary requirements and professional routines.

Woderich (1997) rightly points out that for East German teachers, there were considerable demands of practical day-to-day common-sense action, social responsibility and energy in the transition of school systems, if they were to manage to establish normality, reduce the possible lack of good order and secure basic functions. Döbert (1997) is right to diagnose a tension between the external reconstruction, which led from restructuring to a new school system, and the internal reform, which may have been laid down in laws and curricula, but had to be carried out by a teaching body which had first to find its new roles in a new system. Processes of social adjustment and resocialisation began in the new structures, which were experienced as, in some ways, as radical as the induction and accommodation process at the start of a professional career – 'praxis shock'. The case study above is also evidence for this.

Through our case analyses, we can demonstrate that teachers, after a somewhat intensive experience of loss of confidence, adapted increasingly to the new system, accepted it and increasingly developed it. The basic attitude, which could be seen in their past, of accommodation to requirements was helpful in this, and led to a surprising degree of professional satisfaction. This position was and still is of great importance for the school to be able to function, but has an ambivalent relationship with more recent school concepts of self-responsible participatory school development. Whereas official requirements are carried out dutifully, self-generated activity and self-responsibility for school development are less highly developed.

The predominant coping strategy in a transition fraught with fears of doing something wrong was *to revert to familiar habits.* This applies particularly to organisational regulations in schools as well as for classroom teaching methods. It made it possible to overcome uncertainties relatively quickly. But in many ways, it distorted vision of opportunities and needs for the inward school reforms, which should go beyond new requirements to update and depoliticise curricula and lead to new forms of pedagogy and school life.

To exemplify this, let us consider one problematic area of interpretation which we worked on. As a result of many patterns of argumentation, we take it as read that the teachers (especially those who are strongly subject-oriented [logotropes]) feel responsible for pupils' results. This internalised sense of responsibility probably has, in addition to elements of individual professional ethics, its roots in the basic notion of the teaching role infused by GDR didactics and – probably even more significant – in basic institutional requirements. With these, the teacher had to take responsibility if pupils produced poor results, if too many low marks were given for prepared work, if pupils had to repeat the year, etc. To this extent, there was a burden of proof and accountability reinforced by centralised school leaving examinations and the *Abitur.*

This view of responsibility for pupil's results is underpinned and reinforced both by an understanding of what is 'academic' and by social responsibility for the pupil ('not to have anyone repeat the year', 'to help them achieve leaving qualifications'). So, in the given institutional context, both the academically oriented and pupil-oriented teacher come to the same conclusion: they must achieve clear, measurable knowledge targets, and, whether for the sake of the topic or of the pupil, it is the teacher's duty to make good any knowledge deficits.

Such thinking about responsibility has consequences for the shaping of classroom teaching. The teacher must check and recheck individual results in different ways. Cooperative forms of working make this difficult. This feeling of personal obligation to monitor also has consequences for the presentation of a lesson. It usually begins with oral recapitulation or testing of homework, together, perhaps, with a 'daily exercise' which is similarly amenable to testing. This is where, *vis-à-vis* targeted learning content, deficits or grey areas usually show up. These are interpreted by the teacher (as responsible for results and as the expert on what knowledge is right, but also as the supporter of weak pupils) as a signal to correct. Phases of going over the work again frequently lead directly to teacher-centred episodes of question-and-answer and supplementary explanations by the teacher, with the sole function of correction. These episodes often last longer than planned.

A further unintended side effect is that time to work on new material is cut. More demanding ways of working, such as group learning, are anyway severely obstructed by 45-minute lesson changes. This mechanism also leads to constant pressure of lesson content. In terms of lesson structure, it favours the traditional 'normal form of whole class teacher-centred lessons'. This form provokes pupil tactics aiming to minimise the amount of lesson content to be covered: what has not been worked on in full cannot be included in the next test of prepared work.

Taking responsibility for pupils' results leads to a greater emphasis on measurable cognitive knowledge rather than capabilities and competencies. To build up capabilities and competencies generally requires more time and they are more difficult to measure. Furthermore, in relation to the centralised examinations, standards have to be attained which are likewise predominantly perceived as reproduction of knowledge. Thus, there arises the danger that the instructional function of teaching is emphasised and the task of developing problem-solving capabilities and competencies is neglected. In terms of standards to be attained, creativity and cooperation are incompatible, obstructive and unsettling.

The new demands (key qualifications, key problems, individualisation, cross-curricular learning, project and group work) fail to be met by the teaching patterns, which tend to be internalised.

Here it should be noted that not all teachers operate undifferentiating methods in accordance with this thought pattern. We have recorded a higher degree of openness to alternative teaching procedures among those teachers who were already using mixed teaching methods in GDR times and not just accommodating to the 'norm' of whole class teaching from the front, and who were also on the way to shaking off formal prescriptions. They were already developing their own aims, giving themselves scope and using it. Their interpretation of currently available scope is different from that of those teachers who had absorbed the 'pedagogy of inculcation' and internalised it with their thought patterns.

Against this background there arises a difficult problem for future processes of internal school reform: images to inform action for change in classroom teaching are absent, as well as collegiate staff perspectives which would underpin change and the pedagogical competencies required for it. There is also a general absence of motivation for change in classroom teaching, since important factors which encourage focus on knowledge and achievement are perpetuated in the continuing institutional requirements, in the very foundations.

Implications Beyond the Context of Research

Even though there are limits to comparability of these processes, we are persuaded that our methodological approach in general and also particular conclusions drawn by us could contribute to a better understanding (both by external experts and in the countries themselves) of reconstruction processes in other formerly communist societies of central and eastern Europe and of the attitudinal patterns of the actors involved. Our approach and findings can also be adopted in the sense of a basis for comparison for comparative cultural studies in which the significant cultural and historical background patterns are worked out for a particular region (for example, in Russia, the Perm region), so that the prerequisites are created for a culture of cooperation and reform, not aimed merely at adaptation of existing concepts and structures of Western hue, but defining both the institutional or organisational structures and also the biographically and collectively acquired patterns of attitude and concept of those who are engaged on the spot, to provide a foundation and starting point for developments which are process-oriented.

We consider the design we have adopted to be applicable for the analysis of the starting situation, and also as a form of scientific evaluation to accompany processes of reform or development. Linked to feedback of results to inform further programmes of initial and in-service training, we consider the work with case studies to be particularly productive in programmes for the continuing professional development of teachers. As our experiences have shown, it is case studies, above all, which contribute, over and above the confrontation with unfamiliar perspectives or indeed the resolution of one's own case to a heightening of self-reflection and of competencies for interpreting situations and for practice.

A design along the lines of our project proposal, for external, research-based evaluation of school development processes, teacher training programmes etc. could then be linked to professional development programmes, aimed especially at competencies of self-evaluation for the school-based actors. But there are also promptings for reflection in the methods used for collecting evidence, and this we had not particularly anticipated. Many teachers made the point that they had thought again about things long afterwards, and that this did not surface in the daily round. One school even considered whether every teacher should have the opportunity of a video confrontation once a year. The range of positive views expressed about the video confrontations was so wide that we will summarise them here in three points.

First, the video recordings enabled many teachers to see themselves as personalities from the outside, and to reflect on otherwise unnoticed behaviours (mime, gesture, voice, language etc.) Also, when free from the direct pressure of teaching activity, they found it easier to see teaching and learning processes from several perspectives – including pupil perspectives – and to investigate them. And finally, many teachers were able to gain insights into previously unrevealed action points and corners of the classroom. The recorded lessons made it possible to give attention to phases, situations, locations and persons otherwise only peripherally noticed, if at all. Depending on the nature of the aspects they picked up, all this provoked a variety of reactions among teachers, ranging from self-assurance to insecurity. But what all these reactions have in common is that they are part of teachers' self-reflection.

Notes

[1] For a more detailed exposition of the project, see Wenzel (1995, 1996).

[2] Our chosen interview procedures for the video confrontations are modelled on Breuer (1995).

[3] Included in the sample were 18 teachers (13 women and 5 men) from different pre-Wende school types, from various current school types (6 'secondary', 6 gymnasium, 6 'comprehensive'), and from different subject areas (mathematics/science, language/humanities).

[4] Gymnasium: the 'academic' or 'selective' secondary school model to age 19 adopted from many West German Länder.

[5] EOS: the GDR school extension 16-19, to pre-university and training entry.

[6] SED: the GDR Socialist Unity (or Communist) Party.

[7] POS: the GDR basic 'polytechnical' school, age 6-16.

References

Breuer, F. (1995) Das Selbstkonfrontations-Interview als Forschungsmethode, in E. König & P. Zedler, P. (Eds) *Bilanz qualitativer Forschung. Band II: Methoden*, pp. 159-180. Weinheim: Deutscher Studien Verlag.

Döbert, H. (1997) Zur beruflichen Um- und Neusozialisation ostdeutscher Lehrerinnen und Lehrer, in: S. Buchen, U. Carle, P. Döbrich, H-D. Hoyer & H-G. Schönwalder (Eds) *Jahrbuch für Lehrerforschung, Band 1*, pp. 77-102.Weinheim: Deutscher Studien Verlag.

Fuhrmann, E. (1996) Zur Neuorientierung des Lehrens und Lernens unter veränderten schulischen Rahmenbedingungen, in: W. Helsper, H-H. Krüger & H. Wenzel (Eds) *Schule und Gesellschaft im Umbruch, Band 2: Trends und Perspektiven der Schulentwicklung in Ostdeutschland*, pp. 137-159. Weinheim: Deutscher Studien Verlag.

Händle, C., Nitsch, W. & Uhlig, C. (Eds) (1998) *Lehrerinnen und Erziehungswissenschaftlerinnen im Transformationsprozess. Anhörungen in den neuen Bundesländern*. Weinheim: Deutscher Studien Verlag.

Harms, G. (1992) Lehrerinnen und Lehrer zwischen Verunsicherung und Reformzuversicht, in: Pädagogisches Landesinstitut Brandenburg *Schulreform und deutscher Einigungsprozess. Berichte über eine Fachtagung im Pädagogischen Landesinstitut Brandenburg* am 9./19, pp. 11-19.

Huberman, M. (1989) The Professional Life Cycle of Teachers, *Teachers College Records*, 91, pp. 31-57.

Krause, G. & Wenzel, H. (1998) Lehrerbewusstsein und Handlungsstrukturen im Wendeprozess, *ZfPäd*, 44, pp. 565-581.

Pachocinski, R. (1996) Die Schulentwicklung in Mittel- und Osteuropa – Trends und Perspektiven, in: W. Helsper, H-H. Krüger & H. Wenzel (Eds) *Schule und Gesellschaft im Umbruch, Band 1*, pp. 214-234. Weinheim: Deutscher Studien Verlag.

Wenzel, H. (1995) Lehrerbewusstsein und Handlungsstrukturen als Voraussetzung für die pädagogische Schulentwicklung in den Schulen der neuen Bundesländer, in: J. Keuffer (Eds) *Diskurse zu Schule und Bildung* (Werkstatthefte des Zentrums für Schulforschung und Fragen der Lehrerbildung), Heft 4, pp. 88-121. Halle: Universitäts- und Landesbibliothek Sachsen-Anhalt.

Woderich (1997) Ich mag Schüler trotzdem noch. Fallanalysen zur Verarbeitung biographischer Unsicherheit, in: S. Buchen, U. Carle, P. Döbrich, H-D. Hoyer & H-G. Schönwälder (Eds) *Jahrbuch für Lehrerforschung, Band 1*, pp. 149-172. Weinheim: Deutscher Studien Verlag.

Wenzel, H. (1996) Zur Spezifik der Schulentwicklung in Ostdeutschland, in: W. Helsper, H-H. Krüger & H. Wenzel (Eds) *Schule und Gesellschaft im Umbruch, Band 2: Trends und Perspektiven der Schulentwicklung in Ostdeutschland*, pp. 20-28. Weinheim: Deutscher Studien Verlag.

Wenzel, H. (1998) Neue Konzepte zur pädagogischen Schulentwicklung und die Qualifizierung der Akteure, in: J. Keuffer, H-H. Krüger, S. Reinhardt, E. Weise & H. Wenzel (Eds) *Schulkultur als Gestaltungsaufgabe*, pp. 241-260. Weinheim: Deutscher Studien Verlag.

Zymek, B. (1992) Historische Voraussetzungen und strukturelle Gemeinsamkeiten der Schulentwicklung in Ost- und Westdeutschland nach dem Zweiten Weltkrieg, *ZfPäd*, 38, pp. 941-965.

Zymek, B. (1996) Der Stellenwert des deutschen Einigungsprozesses in der Bildungsgeschichte des 20. Jahrhunderts, in: W. Helsper, H-H. Krüger & H. Wenzel (Eds) *Schule und Gesellschaft im Umbruch, Band 1: Theoretische und internationale Perspektive,* pp. 29-47. Weinheim: Deutscher Studien Verlag.

Shared Learning from Shared Experiences

INES BUDNIK & HARTMUT WENZEL

Introduction

The TEMPUS–TACIS Project, 'Developing Teacher Training for Special Educational Needs at Perm State Pedagogical University (Russia)', on which we are reporting now, has been formally completed as far as the EU financing is concerned – but in reality it is still alive. New courses started a few weeks ago. Since the impact of the project so far can be seen, we believe that the project has been successful, and the evaluations point in the same direction. As of September 2000, we are at the beginning of a new 3-year project. This new project is on health education. It is a result of the former project. In speaking to practitioners for special education in the participating schools, health problems were shown to be a major cause for special needs. So now we are in between two projects and the Edinburgh European Conference on Educational Research has given us a good opportunity to reflect, discuss and reconsider some of our experiences. We hope that this will be worthwhile not only for the future project but also for other projects in eastern and central Europe which are now in an interesting and quite complex transformation process.

These reflections are still personal reflections. They are based, on one hand, on the experiences of the former project, but, on the other hand, on the special personal and historical background of members of an East German university which experienced Soviet influence and underwent a similar societal, ideological and scientific change throughout the last decade. So, Halle University in a certain sense could play a bridging role within the former project and perhaps in the new one as well. We still have personnel at our universities who worked together with Soviet scientists, even studied at Soviet universities for a certain period, who learned Russian as a first foreign language and who then became acquainted with Western ideas after 1989.

The TEMPUS-TACIS Project we are reporting on lasted from 1996 until 2000. The coordinator was John Sayer from the University of Oxford. The other university partners were and are the universities of Amsterdam, Perm and Halle. Since we at Halle went through similar experiences with societal and economical transformation processes, we are very much aware of opportunities and problems.

Now we will try to outline some important dimensions of transformation processes. These dimensions are mutually dependent and may be considered as a system. First, some basic principles of our work will be described, which we believe helped to make the first project successful. They are shown in a certain order of progression, or phases of work, which we think to be very important, because a project as a whole, or individual members, may fail if the expected changes are forced to happen too quickly, if sudden success is expected or if a project comes to an end too fast.

Dimensions of the Transformation Process

We put the dimensions of the transformation process which we believe to be important in a certain order. But, of course, they are interchangeable, as shown in Figure 1

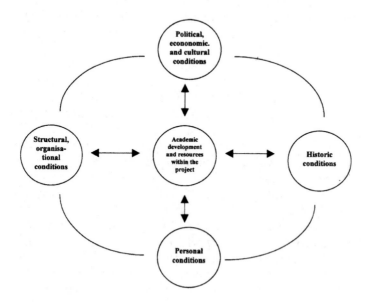

Figure 1. Dimensions for transformation processes within the Tempus project.

Within the development of training units for SEN at a university, all these dimensions have proved important and have been included in the development process, and therefore were influential.

Academic Development and Resources within the Project

The project was organised and set up at the State Pedagogical University of Perm. The main objective of our efforts was to establish a curriculum to qualify teachers for children with SEN. Goals of the project were:

> support for establishing a new interdisciplinary faculty for teacher training in the field of special education, developing the needed course work, including in-service training programmes, and providing sufficient resources;
> support for establishing a network including the university, institutions for special education and regional political agencies; and
> support of the curriculum development and funding (Tempus-Tacis, 1998).

In order to achieve sustainability of the project, we tried to build up a lasting and stable regional support system.

Political, Economical and Cultural Conditions

Of course, the political, economic and cultural conditions of a country in which a project is launched have to be taken into consideration, as well as the region (the regional unit) and the local community. Within our project, it has always been important to know about the economic situation, about the politics and culture of Russia, and to keep this in mind in planning activities. The size of the country, the political structures and the specifics of the region required us not just to consider Russian mentality and thinking but also to deal with special regional features. The Perm region is as big as France, but has only 3 million inhabitants; it is an area with little infrastructure and – that is very important – it shows that schools are very often the main intellectual, political and cultural centres. So, they can be looked on as major agents for social and cultural changes. This has been partly successful in our project. Admittedly, the priority of practical project work took place with schools in the city of Perm but close cooperation could be developed with the agency responsible for the Perm region, Deputy Director of Education, Galina Gutnik. Towards the end of the first TEMPUS project, a new course for teachers in special education from the Perm region had just started. The economic and financial situation of Russia, the Perm region and the city of Perm provide the framework of conditions for resources and funding. We therefore could not carry out all the ideas of the Western partners within the time we had (for example, an electronic network for all schools with special education).

We were able, however, not just to establish contact with the city and regional authorities but also to win their support for the project. Through discussions and study visits in Western partner countries, we have been able to develop political support for necessary changes in attitude and policy.

Historical Conditions

The historical conditions can be shown on two levels. On the first level are the social conditions. But at the same time, one has to mention the scientific traditions and their historical background. The Martin-Luther University has been able to make an intensive contribution to these two levels. The crossover from the socialist system to the capitalist system in the area of the former German Democratic Republic has been made with such an intensity that the complexity of the experiences cannot be shown here as a whole. Just a few may be mentioned as examples.

Educational science has always been a supporting pillar of a particular society. Changes within society bring out changes in the education system. These changes always have to be carried out by the person who carried out the earlier changes. This is a process which is definitely threatening for this person because he or she questions their own personal history. This threat can only be dissolved by recognition of their work, by high sensitivity and by motivation for changes. Sensitivity can be gained by knowledge of historical conditions and by scrutiny of the history of the discipline within one country.

For our project, it was important to know the development over decades of the Russian special education pedagogy with its clinical orientation. Some major facts can be outlined at this point.

1. Within Russian/Soviet defectology, it was thought that handicaps are always caused by pathological disturbances/deficits; social causes were mostly ignored. The 'communist ideology pictures a picture of a happy, healthy society in which handicaps do not fit' (Perm Regional Department for Education, 1994, p. 6). The one-sided clinical interpretation, even to the extent of repression of handicaps out of the social consciousness, moulded views of the population and of specialists.

2. Children with developmental 'deviations' have been only the object of *public care* and they have been highly segregated (cf. Malofeev, 1998; Korkunov et al, 1998) in large boarding schools. The consequences of this separation cannot be comprehended in their whole dimension, yet Malofeev and Korkunov have named, for example, the following independently from each other:

because of the separation, a consciousness within society was created that handicaps do not belong in the life of that society;

because of the centralisation of special pedagogic institutions, regional education policy was not confronted with handicaps and was therefore not able to acquire competencies in dealing with handicaps;

because of centralised *public care*, families gave their children with handicaps to the state boarding schools; a life with those children happened only *rarely*;

because of the few centralised *boarding* institutions – probably because of the size of the country and the scant acceptance of handicaps – there were only a few experts. Only 9% of all teachers at special education schools in Russia had a special education qualification in 1998 – in Perm, 10% of the pedagogic staff are in special education schools.

3. Because of the highly clinical explanation of handicaps and concentration on recognition of ability for education, all children with minor or medically unverifiable handicaps and children who were not able to handle the demands of a school in one way or another fell out of the special pedagogic education system. The word 'handicap' has been looked at in a very restricted way.

Out of these highly summarised fields of problems for our project group, some short-term assignments resulted in the creation of a *system of terms* according to handicaps. It is understandable that the complexity of changes, whether in a textual, ideological, structural or economic dimension, does not lead in the short term to an optimal solution, particularly because the changes are made by people whose attitudes and consciousness are also subject to long-term changes (cf. Sannikova, et al, 1999).

Structural-organisational Conditions

Qualification courses for SEN teachers were established at the Perm State Pedagogical University, but it was a fact for all participants that the courses should not run in isolation from already available structures. So, the project gave special emphasis to the development of a network of all participants.

This means:

the training of qualified special education teachers also includes transformation processes at schools embracing SEN. A project for scientific qualification of pedagogues must include practice at schools in all areas;

every region already has its structures for in-service training for teachers. These structures must be examined and integrated with the project in the right way;

qualified special education teachers are already working within institutions. Even if they seem to be tied into particular channels of development, they should be involved in the project. Ignoring them while working would be counter-productive;

all institutions and persons having contact with the working field should be involved in the development process. If this is effective, many changes can be initiated at many levels.

In Perm, we were able to built up a common network of university, practice, education policy and in-service training institutions, and therefore a concept for training and in-service training for special education teachers could be constructed.

Personal Conditions

Within this dimension, we also have to look at different levels.

(a) An international joint management group focuses on as many main areas as it has members. The development of a consensus within the group has been and still is a condition for successful work, so that variety means enrichment.

(b) If at a university new fields for studying are opened up, new jobs for academically qualified employees cannot be opened automatically. And it is a fact that the number of academics for the field of special education pedagogy in Russia is fairly small. Within this project, an interdisciplinary core group was founded, including academic staff from the University, from teacher training institutions and qualified pedagogues. Their main effort was self-qualification for the new area of teaching, for the development of a curriculum and for realisation of courses.

(c) It has been necessary to introduce young graduates to this academic field in order to create durable fields of study. As one possibility, PhD courses have been used. Young, pedagogic graduates talented in languages were offered the opportunity of a PhD course in one of the Western partner countries. For those young scientists it will be easier to achieve the academic transfer.

(d) In a limited number also, guest inputs, workshops and courses have been offered. These events are useful if they function as *multiplier training*. But if they had been seen as single events without follow-up effects, they would have contradicted one important working principle of the project: All helping actions have to initiate self-powered actions; they must be help for self-help.

Principles of Work

The following principles have not been explicitly formulated for our project or laid down as a codex. They rather influenced as a common approach the whole work of the joint management group.

1. The essential substance for all participants was probably that all ideas and support from all participant countries were seen as an offer. The realisation of these offers, the selection of the foreign models for one's own conditions, could have only be done by the Russian pedagogic educators themselves. Therefore, the first *principle* of the work can be formulated as *help for self-help.*

2. Closely connected to this has been the essential substance of respect for work put in and faith in the will for achievements. Since changing consciousness is a long-term process, even small results are a great success. Wrong expectations and pushing in particular ways paralyse the processes of self-organisation. Faith in this process does not mean blind faith. The development of fear-decreasing and activating evaluation criteria does not contradict the *principle of respect and faith.*

3. During the whole work, the University was not the only focus of our efforts. The development of a network with all dimensions of the transformation processes can be included in the *principle of entirety.*

4. The smooth flow of information between the different levels and dimensions was difficult, but necessary. Only the same information level could guarantee the same starting conditions. Because of the plurality of all participants, a large number of different goals and working expectations had to be united. This working method can be described as the *principle of steady information and consensus development.*

Many working methods were so natural that they hardly needed to be verbalised.

Working Phases of the Project

The working phases themselves are defined through the programme of the project. In the mid-1990s, every project had a pre-project phase (Pre-JEP). It can be decisive for the success or failure of a project. In Figure 2, individual phases and their contents are shown.

Pre-JEP Phase

This first phase is necessary in order to establish contact with each other. The joint management group needed to find a common basis for working. Another meeting in Perm was necessary for grasping individual dimensions of the development process, for initial information about these dimensions, and for exploring which networks seemed to be feasible. This phase is especially important to find out terminological differences which have to do with thinking systems, that can lead to communication problems. Therefore, the Pre-JEP phase is important for textual communication. The main content of the Pre-JEP phase was the development of a working programme, as a flexible programme which reacts to changing conditions and which includes evaluation criteria at the same time. These evaluation criteria were set up by a subgroup of the joint management group. Its members also took care of the documentation of all events. Another very important function of the Pre-JEP phase is the commitment to the framework of conditions and the planning of management. Summarised, the Pre-JEP phase is necessary to pre-plan development lines which can only be corrected with huge effort.

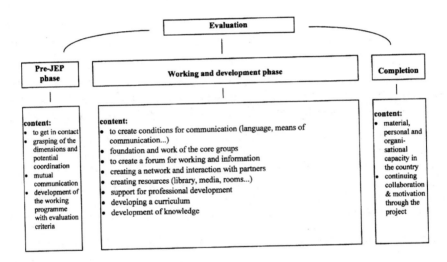

Figure 2. Working phases and the content within the Tempus project.

Working Phase

Within the working phase, it was important not to concentrate one-sidedly on the establishment of university courses but to support contextual analysis on a broad basis. Within the core group at the Pedagogical University, experiences of study trips were evaluated, possibilities of transferring into one's own region were examined, the curriculum was developed and organisational frame conditions were set down. The core group has continued to be the regular contact of our joint management group. Authorities of the University, practical persons from schools, from in-service training institutions and from the regional education policy-makers were members of the core group.

With the help of the core group, a team of teaching profession students was formed with English and German language as their main area. This team had two assignments. First, it had to do extensive translation work because linguistic conditions were not adequate everywhere. Second, for one part of the team, interest grew in the topic of special education teaching. These students had ideal conditions for a postgraduate degree in the partner countries. Therefore, the student teams had the function of supporting linguistic communication and they were also a source for the development of staff. During the working phase, a TEMPUS room at the University was created, which could firstly be used for discussion and secondly, accommodated international literature and modern media for the project. This material base of the project was accessible for all participants of the courses. Of course, it cannot be expected that all the literature is processed according to language in such a way that it can be used by all the participants. But part-translations were also made through the interpreter team.

The qualification courses are designed with work-related fields of study. Therefore, a direct transfer was made into the practice of schools. The effort to change the practice at school according to new knowledge has been supported by the local educational service because their members have been integrated into the whole working process.

Through the core group, through representatives of education authorities and through the joint management group, opportunities were created for the exchange of experiences of school practice and university work. Because of the international dimension of the work, wide public interest was aroused. This had a positive effect on the motivation of all participants but also had importance related to the raising of awareness in the social area.

International conferences, workshops and discussions have been a forum for information exchange. A local journal in which schools document their changing processes has been published in Perm. The entire work has been done with so much intensity and commitment that the completion of the project was connected with fear for many participants.

Completion, Self-engagement

A project is successful if it can be realised within its own material, personal and organisational means. Experiences in Perm showed that this is possible. But this is not to recommend that a project should simply close after the allotted period of time or that all contacts should be broken. Especially in the difficult work of special education, it is helpful if public interest is sustained by visits from other countries.

Therefore, sporadic work visits and international conferences are of importance. Resources should be provided for this. Follow-up support through the joint management group should also be there, in keeping with the development of employees. This was made possible through the organisation of scholarships for PhD study and supervision of doctoral dissertations on the one hand, but on the other hand, scientific discussions for young academics and pedagogues in Perm would be very helpful.

Summary

The success of the completed TEMPUS–TACIS project makes it possible to generalise these experiences. At this point, it is necessary to say that two major components have not been mentioned. But they are also essential. On one hand, there was the competent, sensitive project management, carried out with dignity, respect and tolerance. And on the other hand, there was the entire working climate, which did not just concentrate on the subject and was not just made of working contacts but where the human being could unfold as a whole. The inclusion of the aspect of living experience had a positive influence on the working climate.

The common work of university, regional and city policy and school practice showed results beyond what could have been anticipated at the beginning of the project. It has always been emphasised that ideas from foreign countries have been received with interest, but that problems have to be solved alone and that the readiness must be there.

References and Further Reading

Budnik, Ines (2000) Zu Transformationsprozessen in der russischen Sonderpädagogik am Beispiel Perm, in S. Ellger-Rüttgardt, S. Dietze & G. Wachtel (Eds) *Sonderpädagogik und Rehabilitation auf der Schwelle in ein neues Jahrhundert*, pp. 292-296. VHN (69 Jg.) 9-2000. Universität Fribourg.

Budnik, Ines (2000) Opp, Günther; Puhr, Kirsten: Transformationsprozesse in der schulischen Erziehungshilfe in Sachsen-Anhalt seit 1989, in S. Ellger-Rüttgart & G. Wachtel (Eds) *Zehn Jahre Sonderpädagogik und Rehabilitation im vereinten Deutschland*, pp. 267-278. Berlin: Luchterhand.

Hoffmann, D. & Hoffmann, I. (1998) Das russische Sonderschulwesen im Prozeß der Umgestaltung des Bildungssystems, *die neue Sonderschule*, 43, pp. 199-209.

Kolesnikov, A. & Sayer, J. (Eds) (1999) *Obutchenije detej so spezialnymi nushdami*. Perm: Perm State Pedagogical University.

Korkunov, V.V., Nigayev, A.S., Reynolds, L.D. & Lerner, J.W. (1998) Special Education in Russia: history, reality, and prospects, *Learning Disabilities*, 2, pp.186-192.

Malofeev, N.N. (1995) Sovremennoe sostojanie korrekzionnoj pedagogiki, *Korrekzionnaja Pedagogika*, 3, pp. 3-11.

Malofeev, N.N. (1998) Special Education in Russia: historical aspects, *Journal of Learning Disabilities*, 31, pp.181-185.

Ministry for General and Vocational Education, Russian Federation (1997) *O spezifike dejatelnosti spezialnych (korrekzionnych) obrasovatelnych utchreshdenij I-VIII vida*. Regulatory Circular, Moscow, 4 September.

Ministry for General and Vocational Education, Russian Federation (1998) *O dopolnenii peretchnja tipov u vidov gosudarstvennych i munizipalnych obrasovatelnych utchreshdenij*. Regulation Nr 15/368-6, 8 Oktober.

Ministry for Education, Russian Federation (1992) *Ob utvershdenii primernovo poloshenia o klassach kompensirujuschtevo obutchenija v obschtcheobrasovatlenych utchreshdenijach*. Regulation Nr 333, 8 September.

Perm Regional Department for Education (1994) Konzepzija Rasvitie spezialnovo obrasovanija v permskoij oblasti (Development policy for special education in the Perm Region).

Sannikova, A., Kosharskaja, V., Oslon, V. &Greft, S. (1999) Professionalnaja podgotovka utchitlejei k rabote s detmi so spezialnymi obrasovatelnymi nushdami, in A. Kolesnikov & J. Sayer, J. (Eds) *Obutchenije detej so spezialnymi nushdami*, pp. 74-85. Perm: Perm State Pedaogical University.

Sayer, J. (Ed.) (1999) *Preparing Teachers to Meet Special Educational Needs in Russia*. Leuven/Apeldoorn: Garant.

Schweisfurth, M. (2000) Coming in from the Cold: a reflexive account of an outsider researching in Russia, in J. Sayer (Ed.) (2000) *Preparing Teachers to Meet Special Educational Needs in Russia*, pp. 41-55. Leuven/Apeldoorn: Garant.

TEMPUS Joint European Project (1998) *Annual Report & Statement of Expenditure*. Oxford: OUDES.

van der Wolf, K.& Sayer, J. (Eds) (1999) *Opening Schools to All: an international approach to inclusive education in Perm*. Leuven/Apeldoorn: Garant.

Vesti obrasonania goroda Permi (1999). Perm: Education Department.

Information and Computer Technologies in the Russian School

E.K. KHENNER & A.V. KNIAZEV

Some Remarks about Terminology

So long as thesaurus problems exist, before we write about the Russian educational system for a reader from another country, we must try to explain the real content of some terms.

1. All processes which are connected with the development and introduction of information and computer technologies in education, teaching and learning, school management and management on all other levels of the educational system in Russian pedagogical literature are referred to by the collective term 'Informatisation of Education'. We use this term below.

2. The school subject that is analogous (but not identical) to 'Computer Science' or 'Information and Computer Technology' (ICT) we name 'Informatics' or 'Informatics and Information Technology'. We also use these terms below.

3. We name the stages of school education in Russia as primary, secondary and high school; together they include 11 years. The term 'comprehensive school' we also use in common with other countries. The primary and secondary schools are named together 'basic school'.

The History of Development and Introduction of ICT in Common Education since 1985: main directions

In the USSR, the first experiments in using computers in education and in school management began in the 1960s. In specialised schools, a new subject, 'Programming', was taught, and large higher education institutions invented computer management systems. Such activities were not common, however, especially in schools, and were sustained mainly by the enthusiasm of some teachers.

In 1985, with the beginning of perestroika, the first federal programme for the computerisation of comprehensive school education was adopted. It assumed the provision of schools with domestically made computer techniques, and the introduction of a new compulsory subject called 'Principles of Informatics' (which is also known as Computer Science) in high school. It also deals with the development of methodology and software both for that subject and for the gradual introduction of computers into other disciplines.

During 1993-97, the efforts toward 'informatisation' of education in Russia on the federal level were reflected in the Programme of Informatisation of Education. Here are some excerpts from it:

Informatization means much more than just an introduction of a new content and new technologies into the process of education. Today, the level of informatization is characterised by the level of the development of the state in general and its ability to become a member of the global community.

The role of Informatization in the perfection of education is extremely important. Modern resources of Informatization make it possible to accumulate a great variety of methodological materials, make them open for teachers and students, ensure wide use of visual aids and open the ways for individual teaching.

There are the following ways to realise the potential of Informatization:
* providing schools with computers and accompanying techniques, which make it possible to use new information technologies in education;
* educating teachers in the use of the new technologies; working out the necessary educational methodology and materials such as computer programs, printed, audio and visual production;
* the creation of an infrastructure, making educational information open to all educational establishments; the creation of the conditions which would stimulate the development and use of new methods of teaching.

The problems are very difficult, but the ways to solve them have already become clear enough. Informational infrastructure may be set up in the sphere of education on the basis of telecommunication nets and banks of pedagogical information. The creation of educational methodology and materials is supposed to be done not from the Federal Government's funds, but through the transition to a market economy and by setting up an 'electronic exchange'. That means databases, connected with the educational telecommunication net. It is necessary to work out and put into practice the federal standards in informatisation of education. It is also necessary to create a system of official certification of hardware and software, recommended for use in education.

The aims of the programme were the following:

the creation and introduction of educational methodology and materials for putting into practice;
the recommendations of the Basic Education Plan for Informatisation;
the creation and introduction of the educational standard in Informatics;
the creation of a computer educational information net with at least 40 nodes;
the creation of a bank of pedagogical information by each node;
the creation of a state system of certification of hardware and software of the educational informatisation;
the creation of inter-regional centres for the informatisation of education.

Insufficient federal financing of the programme made it difficult to put it into practice. As the entire financing of common education is assigned to the regional budgets, fundamental discrepancies in informatisation have appeared between regions. This is rather typical for modern Russia, but it was not typical at all of the former USSR. Such an approach has both advantages and disadvantages, and only time will show whether it will live long and what its consequences will be.

In 1996, the reform in management of the educational system in Russia was carried out on the federal level. Instead of two federal ministries (common education and higher education) a single Ministry of Common and Professional Education was established (now the Ministry of Education). In 1997, it developed a unified programme of informatisation for the education system of the whole country. Some concrete projects are being carried out now. Their characteristic traits are the attempt to construct a unified system for all sublevels of education and to enlist the universities in resolving problems of informatisation of the school education system.

Technical Base (Equipment, Hardware)

The political and economic problems of recent years have not allowed the programme of informatisation for the school system to be fulfilled completely.

Official statistics for 1995 gave the following data: only 70% of high schools in Russia had computers (average number for one school was 10). If all types of school were taken into account, then only 37% of them had computers for training children (but, of course, the data do not include the schools which had 1-2 computers for management; most educational establishments have that).

Statistics did not give information about types of computers in schools. It is quite realistic to admit that approximately 80% of computers in Russian schools are constructed and produced in Russia, and have poor specifications. For instance, the typical computer, UKNC (of DEC-architecture), register capacity is 16, with clock rate about 1 megahertz, main memory 128 kbytes, monochrome display. The standard local net contains 12 computers and has two floppy disk units. Winchester disk is absent. The speed of data communications in the local net is about 8 kbytes/c. It is quite clear that such a computer makes it possible to tackle only a very limited range of problems of initial computer literacy. It is possible to create a local net where the host-computer is IBM PC and others are UKNC. After that, UKNC are used only as terminals and the software is usually a DOS or Windows program. For example, in the Perm region, there are about 300 such school computer complexes.

A small proportion of our schools in 1995 had computer classes equipped with IBM PCs. In Russia as a whole, there were not more than 20% of them. In addition, Macintosh classes had started to appear in very small numbers. Across Russia, the level of technical equipment at schools was not homogeneous either in quality or in quantity: it varied from nearly 100% in some regions to 20% in others. For example, in Moscow, where the situation is much better than in most other regions, the total number of schools was 1370, of which 1260 were high schools with 1146 computers for educational use. The average number of computers per school was 16. In the Perm region, there were 1439 schools, of which 648 were high schools with 560 computers for educational use. The average number of computers was 12. For a provincial region, the situation in the Perm region is comparatively good. We do not have reliable statistics about the number of schools which had equipment for work in global nets in 1995, but it is realistic to suggest that approximately 2500 schools in Russia regularly used email in off-line regimes and not more than 250 had access to the Internet online.

Starting with 1995, some regions have undertaken drastic reconstruction programmes of old school computers of Russian production, and the supply of schools with modern equipment. The following data are taken from the report of the UNESCO Institute on Information Technologies in Education, 1999.

Total number of schools in Russia: 64,363
Number of schools in rural areas: 12,457
Total number of pupils: 21,500,000
Number of schools with a computer laboratory (not necessarily networked): 25,303 (39.3%)
Mean number of machines in schools with computer laboratories: 12.5

Number of computers in schools: **317,066**

In the Perm region, the mean number of computers in schools is estimated at 12, but some schools are known to have **50-60** machines. About one-half of the computers in schools are described as obsolete (e.g. UKNC, IBM 286 etc.) Almost all of the computers that are used for teaching and learning are networked and offer a Windows environment. About 10% of Perm schools have one access point to the Internet and approximately the same proportion of schools has one or more multimedia systems.

The Subject 'Informatics': role in school education, variants, development and future

In the short period of time between 1985 and 1994, the subject 'Principles of Informatics' developed greatly. Now the third generation of textbooks and educational and methodological materials is appearing. They reflect modern tendencies in the organisation of the course.

Academician Andrey Yershov, the author of the first concept (1985), understood that students would have to study informatics under the conditions of an almost complete absence of computers in schools. This course got the name 'machineless' and could be taught in two variants: with or without computers. The main idea of the course was the development of algorithmic abilities of school children; so-called 'algorithmic thinking'. The special 'Russian algorithmic language' was worked out. The language was very simple and did not have many syntactical limitations. In the presence of computers, it was suggested the course could be completed with elements of programming in Pascal or Basic.

Although today 'machineless informatics' is absolute nonsense, the Yershov course was of great importance in the first stage of school computerisation. Many teachers of mathematics or physics were retrained to become also teachers of informatics. In addition, it created great interest in computers in schools.

In 1988-89, three basic textbooks were published in the subject. The books assumed compulsory use of computers in schools. In the period 1989-95, many schoolchildren in Russia studied informatics through those books. They were written by different groups of authors headed by Kaymin, Gein and Kushnerenko. In the courses by Gein and Kushnerenko, which have much in common, the algorithmic training is realised with the help of special executors: Draftsman, Robot and others. Those executors have a strictly limited choice of commands. And here the influence of LOGO is clearly seen. Programming in Basic and the study of some program sets, such as 'text editors', are also part of the course.

Kaimin's course has a structure that is different from the others and is oriented to mathematical logic and Prolog language. According to the majority of the specialists, this course is not suitable for the ordinary comprehensive school, but it represents a great interest for schools with a mathematics specialisation.

It is probable that for most schools the best course of informatics for beginners in recent years was the course by Gein, Zhitomirskii and others. It has the following contents.

Chapter 1. First meeting with computer
Chapter 2. Algorithm and its properties
Chapter 3. Forks in algorithm
Chapter 4. Circles (repetitions) in algorithms
Chapter 5. Auxiliary algorithms
Chapter 6. Data structures (tables)
Chapter 7. The programming language BASIC
Chapter 8. Character variables
Chapter 9. Informatics as a branch of industry
Chapter 10. Organisation of computer and fields of application

One can see that the algorithmic line dominates in this course

Beginning from 1994-95, the compulsory course of informatics has moved from the high school to the secondary school (that is, the seventh to the ninth forms). The federal curriculum requires a short compulsory course, approximately 70 academic hours. The question of further computer education and its development is left to the local schools' and educational authorities' discretion. In this connection, a heated discussion about the role and content of the course of informatics began again with a new intensity. The result of this discussion was to be seen in some concepts and appropriate teaching materials for students and teachers. The group of specialists in Perm (Semakin, Khenner and Rusakov) developed one such concept. They (together with a group of collaborators) developed and published the necessary teaching materials, such as a manual for pupils, a book for teachers, a special exercise book, and tests for the control of knowledge and skills. Now the Ministry of Education recommends this set of teaching materials for all Russia's schools.

We think that the first part of the course of informatics in secondary school should have a general educational character, and its aim should be to cover all the main sections and directions of modern informatics. The main notion – information and its processing – logically reveals itself later in the course when the student becomes familiar and actually works both with an ordinary packet of programs (such as editors, spreadsheets, databases) and with specially invented programs – 'imitators' (such as electronic mail, TV conference and so on). But the present course has very little place for programming.

One of the features of our variant of the basic course of informatics is the possibility to complete it using computers of a not very high level. In reality, most of our schools are equipped with such computers. Here is the topic planning of this course, for about 70 lessons. They may be given either in one or in two academic years.

1. Man and information
2. First acquaintance with computers
3. Text information and computers
4. Graphics information and computers
5. Informational exchange in computer nets
6. Models and tables
7. Databases
8. Spreadsheets and calculations with computers
9. Artificial intelligence and knowledge base
10. Information and management
11. How a computer works

This course represents the main directions of modern informatics: information; computer technique; algorithmiSation; programming; modelling; cybernetics line; social line; naturally scientific line; mathematical line. These directions show the scientific nature of the course. In correspondence to these directions, the course develops the basic practical skills and intellectual qualities of a person.

A similar basic course may be the basis for much more special courses in high school. We are sure that it is unreasonable to suggest one such course of informatics for all students. It is necessary to have a set of courses of different orientations and different levels. We think that the basic course allows children in high school to study one of several optional courses from the second level: modelling, programming, computer graphics, databases and some others.

Now a new, lively discussion about the future of school informatics is taking place. It is connected with transition to the 12-years school. Some educators see in informatics only technology and try to exclude the theoretical part from school informatics. Other specialists (the authors of this chapter are among them) are sure that it is necessary to bring together and reconcile theory with technology.

Standards of Education and ICT

Before the changes that are taking place in Russia, the question about standards of education was not on the agenda. General education was standardised; that is, it was the same for all the schools in the Soviet Union. There were a uniform curriculum, standard textbooks and programmes in subjects. In reality, of course, education was not and could not be absolutely standardised. The curriculum could not be the same in a Moscow school and, say, a small rural school in the Perm region. The reasons are their different financing, the level of teachers, children's training, etc. But officially, it was believed that education was standardised, except for a small number of specialised schools for gifted children.

When the political reforms began, Russia began to disintegrate, so it ceased to be a unified educational zone. Schools began to ignore the standard, using the weakening of control and the increase of the power of regional authorities. That had both positive and negative consequences. The positive ones are the democratising of education, its movement towards recognising children's' individual interests. The negative ones are the lowering of the level of education because of all the many incompetent experimenters. The victims of that were children. It is becoming a serious problem, for example, for a child to change from one school to another.

The Education Law which proclaimed the establishment of so-called 'Standards of Education' established the compromise. The big problem now is to develop all the complicated structures of such a standard and to incorporate it in a special Federal Act. This work began in 1993; the proposed law was introduced as the bill to the Duma (parliament) in 1997. There are essential disagreements on it in the pedagogical community of Russia.

The important part of that standard is the so-called Basic Curriculum of the comprehensive school. There are several types of curricula practised in general education.

1. The Federal Basic Curriculum is the main federal document. The upper legislative body of the country confirms it.
2. The Regional Basic Curriculum is worked out by regional authorities on the basis of the federal one and is more detailed.
3. The council of the school, based on the regional curriculum, works out the school curriculum. The school can adopt standard curricula.

The federal component ensures the unity of school education in the country and includes those educational fields which have disciplines of cultural and national importance.

The regional (nationally-regional) component ensures the requirements of the education of the peoples of Russia. It includes those disciplines, or their parts, which reflect the national peculiarities of the culture – first of all, the native language and literature. The school component reflects the specific conditions of a particular educational establishment. It lets the institution work out and carry out educational programmes independently.

The structure of a curriculum shows us the importance of giving a fundamental scientific and cultural and technological education, theoretical and practical; it includes variable and invariable components.

It is necessary to distinguish the invariable component of education, which means teaching cultural and national values, and the variable component, meaning personal interests and peculiarities of school children. These components are not independent. As a result, there are three main types of subjects in the curriculum of any school:

compulsory, which forms the foundation of education;
compulsory, with subjects self-chosen by the student; and
optional with free attendance.

The Basic Curricula for Schools of the Russian Federation (1998)

Educational fields	Educational components	Number of hours per week													
		I	II	III	I	II	III	IV	V	VI	VII	VIII	IX	X	XI
Philology	Russian as the Official Language	3	3	3	3	3	3	3	3	3	3	3	3		
	Languages and Literature	6	5	5	6	6	5	5	8	7	7	5	5	4	4
Mathematics	Mathematics Informatics	5	5	5	4	4	4	4	5	5	5	5	5	4	4
Society	History Society Geography								2	4	4	5	6	5	5
	Surrounding world		1	1	1	1	2	2							
Science	Biology Physics Chemistry								2	2	4	6	6	6	6
Arts	Music Fine arts	2	2	2	2	2	2	2	2	2	2	2			
Physical culture	Physical culture Safety life	2	2	2	2	2	2	2	2	2	2	2	2	3	3
Technology	Technology Manual labour Technical drawing	2	2	2	2	2	2	2	2	2	2	2	3	2	2
Compulsory self-chosen subjects, optional subjects, individual and small group teaching (6-days school week)		5	5	5	2	5	5	5	5	5	5	5	5	12	12
Maximal load of pupils (6-days school week)		25	25	25	22	25	25	25	31	32	34	35	35	36	36
Compulsory self-chosen subjects, optional subjects, individual and small group teaching (5-days week)		2	2	2		2	2	2	2	2	2	2	2	9	9
Maximal load of pupils (5-days school week)		22	22	22	20	22	22	22	28	29	31	32	32	33	33

Informatics is a compulsory subject for all the country but the regional situation in this area of activity is very different. For example, in the Perm region, informatics is declared as a compulsory subject in years 8-11.

The next level of State Educational Standards is the standard for each educational field. By 'standard of education', we mean the system of minimum requirements which the aims and results of the educational establishments' activities must satisfy. It relates to the activities in the main levels of education: primary, general and secondary school.

The main problems with the elaboration of the subject standards are as follows. The school teachers worry that the requirements set by the standards may be too high for students' preparation, which may be used by the administration against the teachers. There is a danger of turning the standards into a way of taking away the school's freedom. That may slow down the ongoing process of democratising the educational system. These fears are not groundless. Fixing some minimum requirements for instruction (for example, in mathematics) for the whole country, the standard is the same for all parts of Russia, a large and not homogeneous country. Some regions (towns, schools) have already reached the standard. Others will not reach it even in a few years. And in both cases, it will be a useless (even harmful) instrument in the development of education.

There are now projects on the federal components of educational standards for all subjects, which are included in the Federal Basic Curriculum. These projects are approved by the Ministry of Education but they have no status in law. There are essential disagreements about these documents too in the pedagogical community in Russia.

The role of ICT in these projects on standards is low. In reality, most of them do not record it. An exception is, of course, the document about informatics as a special subject (educational field) by Prof. A. Kuznetsov (Moscow, Academy of Education), which includes the following chapters:

common description of the educational field;
aims of education;
place of the field in school curriculum;
cardinal lines of the base course of informatics;
structure of standard;
description of cardinal lines, including compulsory minimum teaching material; and
demands for the level of grounding of pupils (students).

The document picks out the following cardinal lines in school informatics:

information processes;
forms of presentation of information;
algorithms;
computers as performer of algorithms;
modelling;
informational technologies.

It is possible to come to a brief conclusion. This is the standard of the course where fundamental principles of informatics as a science are combined with applications and technologies. One tradition of common education in Russia is its fundamental character, and the document considered above is no exception.

Computers in the Teaching and Learning of School Subjects

The problem of the centralised equipment of software in schools has not been solved. Nowadays, in most of the regions, schools themselves have to search for money to buy educational software. The choice is big enough, but the quality does not always meet the requirements of the educational process. Although the same things are happening in other countries, we cannot say that it is usual. There is no federal system of examination and certification of educational software, which often leads to a waste of resources.

Nowadays computers are mainly used in schools as the technical equipment for the subject 'informatics'. For this purpose, standard programs are used – first of all, the Windows operating system and the Microsoft Office package. In addition, a wide range of special software exists for learning information technologies at the level of elementary education. Such programs as 'RobotLand', and different variants of Logo-like programs are widely used.

At the moment, software is widely used in Russian schools for training in various disciplines, such as chemistry, biology, Russian language, physics, mathematics and foreign languages. A number of companies, such as Physicon, 1!, Tutor and Infoservice-Unson, create the programs for schools.

Consider for example 'Open Physics 2.0', created by the 'Physicon' company. It is intended for use in high schools, lyceums, gymnasiums and colleges. It can also be used successfully for independent physics study and training for entry to higher education. 'Open Physic 2.0' stores complete information on mechanics, mechanical oscillations and waves, molecular physics and thermodynamics. It includes more than 400 tests of different level of complexity, about 1000 typical problems, more than 50 interactive computer experiments, a set of computer labs with problems and questions, plenty of problems of various complexity for independent study, a logfile option, and sound support. It makes it possible to monitor the level of knowledge of a pupil.

Another example is 'The base of ecological knowledge'. It is a polylingual training software complex produced by Infoservice-Unison. As they state, the program is 'historically the first training computer program intended for wide use in the system of continuous ecological education'. It is designed for use in secondary and high schools of different kinds. It contains three sections of different complexity, and covers the topics of food, dwelling, water, energy and natural history among others . The software allows for forming various groups of pupils. It can be done by setting individual problems and modes of work for each of them. It can be used for training purposes and for monitoring. It can generate a detailed logfile during its work. The system uses a graphical interface, and the support of music and speech. It supports different interface languages which can be changed at any time.

It is impossible to give here a full review of the educational software used in Russian schools. The high level of programmers that existed in USSR and continues in modern Russia ensures a high quality of educational software. Most problems in this area are connected with pedagogical ideas (as everywhere).

The TEMPUS-TACIS Project

We will now report on concrete activity that was carried out in Perm State Pedagogical University in connection with the TEMPUS-TACIS project. The development of special programs for children with SEN is a problem of great significance at the present time. We developed a number of educational programs for children with SEN that are based on the original idea that we name 'adaptive interface'.

We have constructed an interface that adapts to the particular users, whether in hand-operated or an automatic mode. In the first case, hand-operated tuning of the interface is processed by the direct manipulation of objects. So, the user can design the interface according to his or her requirements or preferences. In the second case, the software changes the interface in automatic mode using the particular properties of the user. It recognises these properties using a test by the operator.

The adaptive interface is based on the personal physiological properties of the user. Research was conducted on the efficiency of the adaptive interface. It was discovered that the adaptive interface as a rule improves the efficiency of operations by 30% and more. This is also true in the case of pupils with special needs.

We will mention here two programs. The first of them is the simulator of a geographic informational system named GEO-PERM 2000. This program is within a class of complete systems, which make it possible to carry out complex processing of the information during its receiving, storing, updating and presentation. The simulator is able to execute six basic procedures, which are immanent for GEO systems: input, manipulation, management, request, analysis and visualisation. The program also allows the use of peripheral devices and data exchange with a number of widespread software programs during GEO creation. These devices play the role of auxiliary parts of a considered system.

The advantage of this software is its intellectual interface, which makes its use very easy. It can use the scanner and graphic editors for map processing. Manipulations of the cartographic objects and their database links are very easy using this software. Also, the use of a scanner gives a pupil the experience of using peripheral devices. The interface design was carried out carefully during software development. The adaptive interface was developed for the program GEO-PERM 2000. The technology of the adaptive interface is superior in comparison with technologies of the standard user's interface. The adaptive interface significantly expands the users' domain and increases the efficiency of the software. The special users' groups also have this advantage.

The second area of work is connected with a popular direction of pedagogical research today. It is distance education for handicapped pupils (with diseases of the motor system). These people need the new software or modifications of existing software to use the Internet effectively. The user interacts with the software through the interface. Physical and psychological properties of pupils with SEN ultimately determine the interface of the software that is needed. The software must be convenient and easy in use; this is the main criterion.

The program K99a was developed plugging into the Netscape Navigator browser. It implements the virtual keyboard by means of the 'mouse' manipulator. Pupils with special needs can use this virtual keyboard instead of a regular keyboard. The virtual keyboard consists of the set of interactive graphical elements, which simulates the simplest functions of the regular keyboard. The important action during Netscape Navigator use is the process of an URL address input. The only way to implement this action is keyboard use. If the operator cannot do it for health reasons, the virtual keyboard is their last chance. K99a implements an additional service: the option of the interface shape modification. Different elements of the virtual keyboard can be easily moved inside the application window. Also, the operator can change their dimensions. We can describe these options as the implementation of the dynamic interface.

Programs K99a and GEO-PERM 2000 are just two examples of our software built on the same basis. Other examples are our software for mathematics and Russian language study, logical testing, and email software for people with special needs.

Conclusion

The means of introduction of ICT in Russian schools are really the same as in west European countries. Most problems now are connected with economic crisis. Now the country has recovered to the economic position that existed before the profound crisis of 1998, we hope that the financing of computerisation of the system of common education will grow. For example, in 1999, regional authorities in the Perm region purchased about 2000 computers for schools and spent approximately the same amount on other equipment for informatisation. In addition to that, many schools receive such equipment by other channels. The rates of growth in the Russian segment of the Internet are very high; during the first half of 2000, the number of users doubled. Now the Federal Government has announced a programme of total computerisation of rural schools over the next 2 years, connecting most of them with the Internet. Of course, in absolute unit terms, the number of computers is low and most of them are not modern enough, but the methodology of ICT usage in education is developed on a level that is comparable with that in west European countries.

Aspects of Home-School Relationships in a Russian School

ANDREA LACZIK

Introduction

This chapter describes results from a small-scale international study that aimed to investigate home-school relationships in one primary school, in Perm, Russia, and was designed as a pilot study for a larger international comparative study. The overall study is closely linked with the TEMPUS-TACIS project, which has been developing close contacts with the Perm State Pedagogical University (PSPU) since 1996. Although the project is directly linked with the University, it has also built up excellent relationships with local primary 'pilot' schools and the local and regional administration. As a project member, I visited Perm twice before I started to investigate areas of common interest with the TEMPUS project, the relationships between the home and the school. During previous visits to Perm, the TEMPUS pilot schools introduced me to the Russian schools, their organisation, the circumstances they have to work in, staff and school life in general, which was to a certain extent familiar to me already as I come from east Europe myself.

Methodology

In May 2000, I spent 2 weeks in Perm to collect data focusing on home-school relationships in one of the TEMPUS-TACIS pilot schools (School 'A' in the following), investigating teachers' perspectives on home-school relationships and their practice concerning communication with the family. As my research had an exploratory aim, a qualitative approach and research design was developed to reflect this. My main data collection method was semi-structured interviews, but as a supplementary data source, I also used documentary evidence, observation and field notes. I interviewed 14 out of 25 primary school class teachers from the chosen school, two psychologists, the social pedagogue and a deputy head. All of my interviewees were female and the interviews lasted between 25 and 40 minutes.

During interviewing, an interpreter was present to help with the language although simultaneous translation was rarely done, as I have a good passive knowledge of Russian. The questions were always asked in English, allowing the interpreter to translate, to avoid misunderstanding, but the answers were translated only in case of a need for clarification. The interpreters were students of PSPU and studying translation and interpretation skills as their special interest. Stress was put on discussing the aim of the research with them and getting to know them before they became engaged in the work. This was essential in order to minimise possible misunderstanding of the educational jargon as well as introducing them to the research, in which they would play a vital role. In addition to helping with the language, the interpreters also provided useful information about the culture, and about the Russian way of thinking.

School under Investigation – contextual understanding

Contextual understanding is important in order to place the research study in perspective, as is information about the physical environment. What does School A look like and how does it operate?

School A is a 60-year-old, two-storey, H-shaped box building, which is only partly encircled by a fence. There is a small playground, which has a few very simple climbing frames. The school entrance leads to a long corridor, which connects the two wings of the school. On the wall, there are pegs for the pupils' coats, and long benches offer children and their parents a seat. Parents wait here for their children after school. All corridors are painted with oil paint and the floors are tiled.

When entering a classroom, the picture changes. Classrooms are arranged and decorated to create a living-room-like atmosphere. There are display cabinets, many plants, lamps, curtains, sometimes a small rug or an armchair in the corner. The walls are decorated with children's work, photographs from classroom celebrations, or educational material. The middle of the classroom can be viewed as a 'traditional' classroom. There are benches for the children to sit two-by-two, facing a blackboard. The class teacher has a desk and a chair, facing the class. In September, at the beginning of the school year, classrooms are completely bare, with only the furniture in them. The class teacher organises the classroom to become comfortable and pleasant, asking parents for contributions. Every classroom is different and represents the children's, teacher's and parents' imagination. Children call the school their 'second home'. There are some special classrooms such as a language laboratory, separate rooms for the director, the psychologists, and the social pedagogue, and a staffroom.

The student body numbers 625 children in 25 classes. There are 48 teaching staff working in the school. They are all women except for three male teachers. The teaching staff includes the school head, the deputy head for upbringing, the deputy head for educational methods, 24 class teachers, four retired teachers, school psychologists, the social pedagogue, and specialised teachers, for example for physical education, technology and language teaching. Because of the high number of children and the limited size of the school, children go to school in two shifts. Each shift has six 35-minute lessons. The first starts at 8.30 am and finishes at 12.55 pm; the afternoon shift lasts from 1.15 to 5.40 pm.

School A educates children for their first 3 or 4 years at school. Few of its classes follow a 4-year primary compensatory education programme; the majority of classes work according to a 3-year developing education programme. Most of the class teachers are involved in voluntary experimental work led by PSPU academics. Within these initiatives, teachers are free to develop their own teaching programme in addition to the national curriculum. Teachers can choose to develop areas of special interest for their class, such as drama, health and art. At the same time, the school has to deal with real financial limitations. It must very often rely on the generosity of wealthy parents who offer the school financial help, which is earmarked for their children's classes. As a result of the school's good reputation and its programmes for developing education, parents from other school districts are interested in sending their children there.

School A can be characterised as a 'typical' Russian primary school in Perm, yet with unique qualities. In terms of being typical, it is a state school with a non-selective admission policy for children between the ages of 6 and 10 and as such, does not charge tuition fees. The pupils come from different backgrounds, and their families differ in their financial situation, in parents' schooling, in the family structure and so on. The school caters for all abilities, including classes for able children and compensatory classes for slow learners. The school has a highly qualified and committed teaching staff. They are supported and advised by a social pedagogue and psychologists, who, despite economic, social and political difficulties in the last few years, have stayed in the profession. After the major political changes in Russia in 1991, and up to now, the resource level and salaries have been negatively affected, many schools are underresourced and teachers are still badly paid.

Some of the school's unique features made it easier for me to conduct the research. First, School A is one of the TEMPUS-TACIS (Technical Aid Programme) pilot schools. This means that apart from accommodating regular foreign visits, it allows and welcomes researchers and, where it can, makes the most of these. The school head and a few of the staff travelled to western Europe within the TEMPUS Project, where they visited schools, local education authorities and university departments. These visits add to the good reputation of the school and through the experience gained abroad, it has an impact on teachers' thinking and practice. Second, School A built up a very close link with PSPU, its teaching staff and researchers. The school and the majority of the staff are involved in experimental work stemming from the University. Third, School A is located in a residential area close to the city centre and offers easy access for national and international delegations to visit the school. This also has a positive effect on the allocation of resources from the city council. Fourth, within the school's catchment area, there are no opportunities for children to attend clubs and societies, e.g. there are no sports facilities and no House of Culture nearby. For the school, this means providing different after-school activities according to interest to occupy children during their free time. This puts the school under considerable pressure. For these reasons, the school has built up good working relationships with outside agencies, for instance, with the swimming pool, puppet theatre, museums, hospitals, etc. The school itself commented on this as a special feature, unusual in the Russian context, suggesting that other schools do not have to deal with this type of problem.

School A was selected for the study because all of its above-mentioned qualities paved the way for a successful research endeavour. Another important element in choosing this school was that during previous visits, I had already established good personal contacts with the school head and some of the school staff. This certainly helped when gaining access, since I only had limited time for the fieldwork.

Research Findings

I will concentrate on two main themes. One will deal with the understanding of home-school relationships in School A from the teachers' perspectives, the other with different types of existing interaction between the home and school. The research targeted the class teachers' practice and thinking about the relationships between family and school, i.e. the findings are based on teachers' reporting. They are deliberately based on original quotations, enabling the reader to draw ideas from the interviewees' own thinking. The quotations are grouped in order to illustrate the multifaceted understanding of home-school relationships. The examples, mentioned by several teachers, clarify the teachers' views on this issue in School A.

When discussing the research findings, relevant existing literature will also be referred to. Since resource and language limitations make access to Russian literature difficult, publications from other east European countries will be drawn on to supplement the available

Russian publications. Although the articles cannot be handled as a fully representative sample of the existing literature in the field, common themes clearly emerge in addition to unique country-specific issues and approaches. The combination of quotations from teachers and reference to the literature offers a mixture of theoretical underpinning and practical reality in School A.

Concentrating on School A, several teachers described home-school relationships as a cooperation between the school and the family, or as teacher B said, 'We have to work together, the teacher, parents and pupils'. Although this is a broad definition for the terminology, it helps in identifying relevant examples of home-school relationships. The examples that follow include parental involvement in educational issues, such as homework and grades; others are connected with free time or social activities, like school trips or prazdniki (school or family celebrations). This rough picture is far from being complete, but it offers an idea of the issues teachers are concerned with.

Focusing on what teachers said, the interview data clearly show a commitment from the teachers' side to involve parents, where the teachers may have a range of different aims. The teachers consider the home-school relationship important and they believe that all players within it (children, parents and teachers) can benefit from a good relaxed liaison between the home and the school. At the same time, the teachers interviewed showed awareness of the complexity and difficulty of parental involvement.

This generally positive view on enhancing home-school relationships emerges also from the literature. Children's education (Rabušicova, 1995a) and achievement (Safran, 1999) can be enhanced by a good relationship between the home and the school, children can receive a better upbringing if schools and families cooperate (Schüttler, 2000), or talking about children at risk in Poland, students' behaviour and also the family's lifestyle can be affected by communication between the home and the school (Bielecka, 1999). In the former East Germany, the example (Weiler & Mintrop, 1996) points to some schools as clear beneficiaries of a good home-school relationship. These schools can thank their 'existence or status to parents' political lobbying directed against state or local policies' (Weiler & Mintrop, 1996, p. 42).

These views are also demonstrated by the data from this study: all teachers in School A felt that it was important to involve parents and to listen to them. This is indicated by the fact that there is a wide range of activities going on within the school involving both teachers and parents; however, teachers had different attitudes and feelings about their relationship with the parents. As the following examples reveal, they often praised the advantage of a relaxed relationship with the parents, which leads to a happier and better performing child.

> *If the child sees that his/her parents take part in school celebrations, different events, they get on well with the teacher; it is already a pleasant experience. The children consider it as something good and it reduces the 'gap' between the child and the teacher. (Teacher A)*

> *I think it is easier for the teacher to get to know the children if she is in close contact with the family. The family gives the child a lot; these are the basics because the school cannot give everything in education and upbringing. (Teacher H)*

> *I think that parents should be interested not only in children's learning ... And if parents are interested in what is happening at school, what a child is doing at school, not only learning but also what is happening in the class, then the child feels it and his attitude to school gets better. (Teacher H)*

Children's learning and academic achievement is discussed in many publications (Rabušicova, 1995a; Szabó, 2000; Orlova, 1998; Manisheva, 2000). Enhancing the communication and cooperation between the teacher and the parents in order to increase pupils' performance level at school is mentioned as one of the most important aims. Improving children's learning and academic achievement is certainly one of the issues that is in the interest of many parents and teachers, and the two parties often try to communicate with each other in order to contribute to this aim.

While discussing parental involvement in class activities, several issues that highlighted the complexity of the home-school relationships teachers have to deal with arose naturally. These issues were mentioned by teachers because they affected the teacher's everyday practice and reminded them of the changing social circumstances.

> *Parents become more isolated because there is no 'collective' for parents. Parents who belong to a higher social class try to separate themselves from the others. (Teacher E)*

> *If the parents are wealthier, they try to make their children's life more comfortable and they help their children in everything. The celebrations they organise are better and richer. (Teacher B)*

> *In the past parents would come to school very often. Now they have to work a lot to earn their living. They are very busy. (Teacher C)*

[N]ot all the families are complete. In my class now there are many sick children with poor health. (Teacher I)

Now the school tries to do preventive work against alcohol, drugs, cigarettes. (Teacher G)

Parents have got more problems – not with the school but with life itself. Children have less of parent care, have become less looked after. (Teacher C)

The following examples, coming from the teachers, represent their practice and thinking, and their perspectives on home-school relationships. In the process of analysis, it was often difficult to separate perspectives and feelings about home-school relationships, as illustrated in the following quotations:

The relationship must be warm and friendly. (Teacher A)

Some of my personal qualities prevent me from doing this. Some parents are older then I am or are better qualified. Sometimes I find it difficult to work with some parents because of this. (Teacher D)

It is difficult to work with parents together. (Teacher E)

I am worried how much I will find a mutual agreement with the parents, how much we will have common interest in the child's upbringing. To start with I feel fear but when I get to know parents I feel lucky and even years later I keep in touch with them. (Teacher G)

I wish that teachers would be taught how to work with parents. Teachers have to invent themselves and set up the way and method of communication. (Teacher D)

Teachers A, C, D and F see parents in a diversity of roles and address them accordingly:

They ought to give help with the homework if it is necessary. (Teacher D)

I see parents as helpers, not only in learning but also in other activities, like celebrations or other events. And helping the child with their homework. (Teacher F)

109

> *Parents tell me how they can help. Who can saw, or who has good organisational ability. To start with I try to find out the parents' possibilities. (Teacher A)*

> *I encourage them to express all their wishes. They normally write it down for me. What they want and what they can do. For example, somebody can organise a trip or make a presentation for us. (Teacher C)*

Some teachers hand the initiative over to the parents:

> *The main thing is that the starting point is they and not I. ... I only support them in it. For example, they suggest going to the theatre or to go on a trip, or the museum. Or if they don't like something in the classroom and they want to make it look more like home they can suggest buying something. (Teacher C)*

> *In the first grade, I offer parents some options for what road to follow and how to work in the class. So it's either I take the responsibility of teaching only or I also add the responsibilities of organising parents' meetings and extra-curricular activities. (Teacher H)*

The following two examples suggest financial shortages the school or class teacher faces. Teachers handle these issues very openly.

> *Parents offer buying textbooks for the developing education programme. (Teacher F)*

> *On the first meeting I told the parents that I did not like the green walls in the classroom ... So I immediately organised the decoration of the classroom. Everybody added something to it to make it look nice. (Teacher B)*

These quotations demonstrate the different levels on which parents are involved in class matters, and also touch on issues which have an effect on this relationship. It is important to note that teachers have different feelings about working together with parents, which very much depend on their personality, teaching and personal experience. But there are strong similarities in their attitudes towards parents. Teachers showed considerable interest in building up a good relationship with parents, and enthusiasm in involving parents, and many of them valued the parents' information about their children. The data collected strongly suggest that the teachers play a leading role in the evolution of home-school relationships in School A. Most of the time, the teacher is the initiator of contact, trying to involve parents in their children's education and the class's social life. Parents can initiate activities and changes, given that they offer help. These findings are restricted to the teachers of School A. Even in the school itself, a wider range of parental involvement can be discovered when talking to other staff.

Having discussed teachers' understanding of home-school relationships and outlined its complexity, the next part will illustrate a more specific area, the interaction between home and school as seen from the teachers' perspectives.

Interaction in this context is understood as 'communication with somebody, especially while you work, play or spend time with them' and 'when two things have an effect on each other' (*Oxford Advanced Learners' Dictionary*, 2000). The data show clear evidence of interaction between the class teachers and the parents in School A. The data also reveal a pattern in the way teachers and parents interact, but at the same time, I found considerable differences in the intensity of interaction. Part one of this section deals with the interaction during meetings of groups of parents and teachers; the second looks at examples of individual interaction between the home and the school.

The data reveal two fora where the class teacher meets a group of parents to inform or discuss whole-class-related issues. Others might be at present in the school but among class teachers, these two are the most commonly used. The following examples will illustrate the function of the parental committee and the parental meeting. Statements by teachers about the parental committees included the following:

> *There is a parental committee for the class. They organise celebrations, try to involve parents who are not very active. They handle the class budget. (Teacher A)*

> *The parental committee, which is a strong group of parents, suggests and has ideas, what to do, where to go. (Teacher B)*

> *When they choose parents for the parental committee ... There are six people in the committee. Each of them has a certain responsibility, they do everything on their own. Only sometimes, I give a piece of advice. But I do it tactfully and cautiously. They meet when there is a need for it. Now we are preparing for the leaving party. And we meet every week. Because there are many questions to talk over. (Teacher C)*

Another way to get parents together is by inviting them to a parental meeting. Class teachers use parental meetings to inform parents. The agenda and aim of these meetings might be different in each class and their frequency can be regulated by the teacher as necessary. Although every teacher felt that it is an effective way of transferring certain information, the examples that follow will point to the existing differences.

111

> In the first school year, parental meetings take place very often every two weeks. ... It is important that they also get to know each other and it helps to break the barrier ... For the parental meetings I suggest topics to discuss concerning children's learning, without mentioning any names. Sometimes, also, parents suggest themes for discussion. (Teacher D)

> At the first parental meeting, I talk about myself. ... I also ask parents in a written or oral form about what they would like to see in the vospitanie [upbringing]. Together we work out a plan for this. (Teacher A)

> During the academic year, the teacher invites the parents to parental meetings, where she gives advice and recommendations. (Teacher F)

> At every parental meeting, we talk about what is bad and what is good ... If somebody is doing well, I say so, or other cases we discuss in private. (Teacher I)

> Parental meetings are four times a year. These are the main meetings. But in the first year, I organise it more often, if I have some difficulties I can call a parental meeting. But I try not to bother parents. If I need a meeting I ask children to inform parents and we meet. They help me. I have a plan, I work according to it. At the parental meetings, we never talk about children's upbringing. I talk about children to individual parents. Children's progress I also discuss only in private. At parental meetings, we talk about general issues. I invite the psychologist, I invite people who make presentations on what are better ways to help and bring up children. How to develop memory, thinking – so I invite people from outside. (Teacher C)

> I organise regular meetings once a month, which last between one and two hours. Not 100% attend. Because of different reasons. It's hard to find an appropriate time. (Teacher H)

The parental committee and the parental meeting are the fora that almost every class teacher has mentioned. The parental committee is led by a group of parents and their work involves the organisation of social events, trips or theatre visits, etc., for the class. They usually come up with an idea, and after consulting with the class teacher, they try to realise their plan. The class teacher initiates parental meetings and every parent is advised to attend. They are organised regularly and planned in advance. During parental meetings, the teachers avoid discussing individual problems; instead, they concentrate on class-related issues.

In the preceding section, there are two main issues, which are also discussed in the literature. One is the use of parental meetings (Alexeeva, 1997; Orlova, 1998), including the importance of information flow (Rabušicova, 1995b; Füle, 1998; Manisheva, 2000), and the other is the question about upbringing (Phokina, 1998; Bielecka, 1999; Schüttler, 2000; Csapó, 2000).

Parental meetings seem to be widely used, with a broad range of aims. It is evident that not only in School A, but also in the literature, they are considered as an important forum for information exchange between the parents and the teachers. For instance, parental meetings are used to gain and exchange information about the child and their family in order to keep the child's performance level when moving into secondary education (Orlova, 1998). Alexeeva (1997) suggests that good preparation is needed in order to achieve the goal of a parental meeting and suggests that, occasionally, parent groups would meet, and not necessarily the parents of the whole class. Parents need to receive certain information about the school, such as details about the change in the school's daily routine, the school's expectations, price of school meals etc. In addition to parental meetings, Manisheva (2000) reports on the good practice of the open days. She too is concerned with the academic achievement of the child and as a way to report back to the parents, she invites the parents to the open day to visit classes. As part of the open day, there is the opportunity to exchange views, offer advice and recommendations. Consulting other publications, the families are as much in need of information about the schools and the education system (Füle, 1998) as the school about the family (Rabušicova, 1995b; Bielecka, 1999).

Regarding the other common issue, the problem of upbringing needs to be discussed. It is elaborated on in many of the articles, and the teachers are concerned with the same problem. These articles all stress that children's upbringing has to be the result of a cooperation between the parents, the school and the community, where parents play the major part (Phokina, 1998; Bielecka, 1999; Schüttler, 2000). At the same time, it is shown in the literature that different countries do not always have the same practice or the concerned parties do not always share a common view on this issue. For instance, the new 1999 education reform in Poland places the responsibility of the students' upbringing on the school. Bielecka (1999) believes that parents should 'help the school to deal with students whose upbringing causes problems' and they should be asked 'about the course of action which they would pursue in a given situation' (p. 145). Phokina (1998) argues that the development of a human being is so complex that the family can fulfil this task only with the school's help. The school has to reflect the family's morals and cater for it, as the family will help the school in its tasks. At the same time, society has moral expectations of its members, which are expected to be followed, i.e. the society, too, has a great impact on an individual's upbringing.

In the following quotations, attention was given to patterns of interaction between class teachers and individual parents. During the analysis of the interviews, the following patterns of interaction appeared. All interviewed teachers use the *dnivnik* (register) to send written messages or invitations to a meeting to the parents. However, the intensity of the usage of the dnivnik differs from teacher to teacher. Some of them also expect parents to respond through this dnivnik, or others encourage parents to ask questions or to express concerns in it. All teachers felt that it is a quick and effective way of communicating.

> *I write in the dnivnik. I do not write negative things in this.*
> *(Teacher B)*

There are situations when the teacher and parent personally want to talk to each other. The class teacher often invites the parents to school for a confidential discussion about their child's learning or behaviour. These are held on an individual basis.

> *Well, if it is behaviour – and there are such cases as well – if*
> *the problem is serious it's better to go and see parents in their*
> *home. I have a student, this child is completely out of control.*
> *He is intelligent and learning, but lacks self-control. He had a*
> *tragedy in his life before he started school and this affected*
> *him very much. And this child on the first day, on the 1st of*
> *September, beat everybody. I keep in touch with the mother,*
> *we agreed that she would come and see me every week, we*
> *exchanged telephone numbers, she would come to see me and*
> *we tried to solve the problem. (Teacher H)*

> *One of the pupils had difficulty with learning. ... I told the*
> *mother what needs to be worked on. Gave her some additional*
> *material and then I regularly reviewed how they worked.*
> *(Teacher I)*

It also happens that the parent wants to talk to the class teacher, usually because of learning and behaviour or for personal reasons.

> *I do not give any information about achievement until the*
> *moment the parents come and ask for it. So if they need it,*
> *they have to come to school. (Teacher H)*

> *Sometimes a mother comes to me and asks me to be stricter*
> *with her child. Sometimes the child becomes disappointed*

*after a day and the mother comes to school to find out why.
(Teacher E)*

*They often come to talk about personal matters. The child has
got a difficult situation in the family. Mother drinks, there is
no father. There is only grandmother and she brings her up
on her pension money. This grandmother often comes.
(Teacher H)*

*Sometimes, in recent years parents asked for help in
organising a children's summer holiday scheme. We have a
summer camp at school. (Teacher I)*

Teachers had different views on home visits. Some, as the following
examples show, reject it completely:

*When I started working, it was fashionable to go and visit
families, to see how they live, what is their family like. Now I
think it's a private matter. (Teacher F)*

*In the past, primary school teachers used to visit families to
find out about the situation at home. Because parents were not
open. Now – for example in my case – I don't go to visit
parents, they come themselves and talk about everything.
(Teacher I)*

Others make home visits occasionally, with 'good reason', but recognise
the difficulty.

*This can be inconvenient for the family, especially if they have
problems – there is an alcoholic in the family or they are in a
difficult financial situation. I try to inform them if I want to go
and go only to families where there is a problem with the
child. For example: I have a child in the class who could
achieve better then he does. I tried to ring the parents but no
success, so I visited them. Mum got depressed, dad drinks. She
feels that her life is not worthwhile any more ... I try to help
and comfort her. (Teacher A)*

I also talked to one class teacher who still visits families regularly:

*I go to almost to all pupils' homes, sometimes even twice or
three times a year. (Teacher B)*

The views on the appropriateness of the home visit are mixed, listening
to the class teachers in School A. Using home visits as a way of
communication depends on the class teacher's style and personality.

Another effective way of communicating is the telephone. It seems
from the interviews that every teacher has a telephone at home and they

do not mind if parents contact them with their problems in the evening. The majority of parents also have a tlelphone at home, and the class teacher sometimes reaches others through the workplace's telephone.

> *The telephone is a good way to contact parents, practically every family has a telephone at home. That is the first thing I use. (Teacher G)*

> *Most families have a telephone, it is convenient, they can call me at home. If they have a problem or have a question, they can call. For example, a child called me to ask, what is the homework – I asked the child to ring a friend. They can call me if they did not understand what they have learnt today. (Teacher F)*

> *We also solve some problems over the telephone if it's necessary. ... if it is a personal individual matter. (Teacher I)*

Certain teachers send messages with the children, to invite the parents for a consultation:

> *Sometimes I tell the child: 'Please ask your mum to come and see me'. The child does not have to know what it is about. (Teacher B)*

> *Another way of sending messages is through the children. It depends what is more convenient. For example, a child's father was made unemployed and began to drink. The child started to have problems at school. I sent a message to the mother that I would like to talk to her. The mother came the next morning. (Teacher G)*

These examples show that there is interaction between class teachers and parents. They both initiate communication and discuss issues of a personal character, the learning, behaviour or health of the children. Teachers, like parents, have their own preferences of using the written or oral form of interaction, which differs from class to class. Whereas clear similarities can be detected in the ways class teachers in School A interact with the parents, examining the teachers' examples, it is also clear that every teacher uses different means of communication in different situations. The dnivnik is used daily, and it is also supported by the school management. The telephone is generally considered as a quick and efficient way to solve urgent problems, and both the teacher and the parents use it. The data show evidence of personal meetings at school initiated by the teacher or the parent. The list above only outlines some real-life situations, because of which teachers get in touch with parents or the other way round. The list is not exhaustive and the findings only relate to School A.

Conclusion

This article gave an account of 2 weeks' research work in one primary school in Perm, Russia. Teachers in School A seem to think very similarly about home-school relationships. The data suggest that teachers and other school staff consider home-school relationships to be important and, consequently, they all spend much energy and time on improving the relationship between the home and the school. It is also evident that some teachers find it easier to work with parents than others.

According to teachers' reporting, changing social and economic circumstances – the city's, the school's, the family's – introduce them to new professional challenges within this relationship. Teachers showed open-mindedness when dealing with the new situations, although some expressed their wish to receive professional advice in working with parents.

The data suggest that the teachers in School A aim to involve parents in school activities and communicate with them about child-related issues. It was, furthermore, possible to detect and describe unique approaches of teachers in involving parents in their children's education and social activities. The data also show that group or individual meetings are organised by the teacher with different aims. There is considerable flexibility in the frequency and in the way teachers interact with parents and how the way of interaction accommodate individual needs.

The importance of information provided by the school or the class teacher for the parents was stressed as well as the information parents are willing to share with the class teacher about the children and family circumstances.

Although the project was conducted as a single case study and the findings are not generalisable to other primary schools in the region, it offers information about the state of home-school relationships, with their complexity and difficulty, as teachers in School A see it. Keeping this in mind, within the research's limitations, however, the findings can contribute to an understanding of the cultural context and home-school relationships in Russia.

As mentioned at the beginning of the chapter, this was a pilot study for a larger international comparative study. Making the best use of the wide range of experience gained while conducting the pilot study, further research is being developed. Looking at the richness of the data, it is reasonable to suggest another review of it with different foci. This will highlight other home-school relationship issues that School A is concerned with, taking into consideration the views of additional school staff – e.g. deputy head for upbringing, school psychologists, social pedagogue etc. At the same time, almost automatically there emerges the need to investigate this relationship from another angle, from the parents' perspective. In this chapter, the importance of cooperation and communication between the teachers and the parents was clearly highlighted. So far, teachers' thinking and practice has been demonstrated but it is as important to know how parents see home-school relationships and what they have to say about them. This other side of home-school relationships is under current investigation.

References

Alexeeva (1997) Parental Meetings: if they are necessary, for whom? *Director Shkoli,* 29, pp. 29-36.

Bielecka, E. (1999) The School as an Active Partner in Environmental Work? in F. Smith & H. Moerel (Eds) *Building Bridges between Home and School,* pp. 1451-11452. Nijmegen: Stichting Katholieke Universiteit te Nijmegen.

Csapó, B. (2000) Az oktatás és a nevelés egysége a demokratikus gondolkodás fejlesztésében (The unity of education and upbringing in the development of democratic thinking), *Új Pedagógiai Szemle,* 50, pp. 243-244.

Füle, S. (1998) Kritika: Szülöknek az iskoláról (Critics: to parents about schools), *Új Pedagógiai Szemle,* 48, pp. 1231-1225.

Manisheva, G.V. (2000) (Open days for parents), *Nachalnaja Shkola,* 1. pp. 1051-1006.

Orlova, T. (1998) (Entering into a difficult age), *Director* Shkoli, 36, pp. 707-704.

Oxford Advanced Learner's Dictionary (2000) Oxford: Oxford University Press.

Phokina, O. (1998) (Mutual relationships between the school, family and society), *Director Shkoli,* 33, pp. 333-336.

Rabušicová, M. (1995a) Influence of the Family on Educational Achievement, in J. Sayer (Ed.) *Developing Schools for Democracy in Europe,* pp. 125-133. Wallingford: Triangle Books.

Rabušicová, M. (1995b) On Relationships between the School and the Family, in J. Sayer (Ed.) *Developing Schools for Democracy in Europe,* pp. 135-141. Wallingford: Triangle Books.

Safran, D. (1999) Parent School Partnership Programmes to Assist Refugees and Other Vulnerable Population, in F. Smith & H. Moerel (Eds) *Building Bridges between Home and School,* pp. 1531-1558. Nijmegen: Stichting Katholieke Universiteit te Nijmegen.

Schüttler, T. (2000) Csak az együttélésben megvalósuló neveléssel tartható fenn a világ. Kerekasztal beszélgetés a nevelés 21. századi esélyeiröl (The universe is only sustainable by communal upbringing. Round table discussion about possibilities in upbringing in the 21st century), *Új Pedagógiai Szemle,* 50, pp. 455-456.

Szabó, L. (2000) Az iskolának nevelnie is kell (The school should also be involved in upbringing work), *Új Pedagógiai Szemle*, 50, pp. 242-248.

Weiler, H. & Mintrop, H. (1996) *Educational Change and Social Transformation. Teachers, School and Universities in Eastern Germany*. London: Falmer Press.

Emotional Distress and Academic Motivation in Russian and Dutch Early Adolescents

OLGA LEONTIEVA, DMITRI TCHOULAKOV,
SACHA VAN DER GREFT & YANA YEMBOULAEVA

Introduction

For decades, the attention of different social agents has been attracted to adolescents. In the Western world since the 1950s, youth has been treated as a social barometer of societal ills in a wide range of public discourses (see Brannen et al, 1994). It is a common assumption that adolescents are experiencing great changes from physiological (puberty), psychological (identity formation) and social (new social roles and societal expectations) points of view (see Borman & Schneider, 1998; McMahon & Peters, 1990). In Russia, adolescence was and is in the focus of social and, in particular, educational attention. It is stated that this age is strategically important from the developmental perspective: it is sensitive to both positive and negative environmental influences and to a great extent determines future life choices in education, personal and professional life as well as general social orientations (Tsukerman, 1998). That is why this life period is of great importance for school education: it is from here that adolescents either choose the way for fulfilling life in society, or drop out of school and sooner or later are on the fast track to social exclusion.

In general, early adolescence (11-14 years old) is characterised by important developmental changes in psychological functioning and academic motivation. School is perceived as less interesting, valuable or useful; academic competence declines; signs of emotional distress (depressive symptoms, anger, problem behaviour such as school truancy and misconduct) occur more often in comparison with previous developmental periods (Swanson et al, 1998; Roeser et al, 1998a). All these factors hinder school achievement and may cause alienation from school. School underachievement and, as a result, drop-out are in their turn considered to be solid precursors for negative adult outcomes such as social life maladjustment and future unemployment (Evans, 1995). That is why, taking into consideration all the pressures early adolescents experience, the issue of academic functioning and factors reinforcing and diminishing it are seen to be of importance for the organisation of school activities and social services engaged in working with young people.

Unfortunately, the issues of academic and emotional functioning are usually studied in isolation from each other. Recently, researchers have emphasised a need to integrate educational and mental health perspectives on adolescents' development (Boekaerts, 1993; Roeser et al, 1998a).

This chapter has two major objectives. The first objective is to introduce a comparative perspective on mental health and academic motivation in Dutch and Russian early adolescents. The second objective is to examine psychological functioning (namely, emotional distress) and its impact on academic motivation among early adolescents. Applying a comparative perspective to the received data, we intend not only to compare the levels of emotional distress and academic motivation in Dutch and Russian samples that can yield information on the emotional and academic functioning of early adolescents in two different countries, but also to investigate the culture specificity of the relation between emotional distress and academic motivation.

In the theoretical part of the article, we conceptualise emotional distress and academic motivation; we formulate our expectations concerning the levels of distress and motivation in two studied samples, and the ways emotional functioning influences motivational beliefs. Then we describe research instruments and present results. In discussion, we provide possible explanations for the findings and note limitations of the study.

Theoretical Perspectives

Emotional Distress

There is an interesting change of perspective on adolescents' problems in contemporary theoretical and empirical research. From the beginning of the twentieth century until recently, adolescence was supposed to be a period of considerable problems: G. Stanley Hall's 'storm and stress' period, psychoanalytical 'interruption of peaceful growth', E. Erikson's 'normative crisis' and others (see Rutter & Rutter, 1992). Now, there is a growing acknowledgement that it was the number of young people referred for psychological help which influenced such a view on this developmental period. According to research data, the general adolescent population (at least in Western cultures) sustains psychological equilibrium during this time of their lives and copes efficiently with the developmental tasks characteristic of it (Crijnen et al, 1997; Roeser et al, 1998a).

'Nevertheless', as Rutter & Rutter (1992) write, 'the myths were not wholly wrong' (p. 229). For physiological and psychosocial changes do take place and make young people subject to a number of new experiences different from those of the previous life period. It is too early to deconstruct adolescence as a problem period without consistent, multicultural research. Thus, to be accurate, adolescence could be quite a challenge for some young people. The size of this category of adolescents and possible explanations for their specific problems are still matters of further research. In this respect, cross-cultural comparisons could supply some information about the differences in mental health in different cultures.

Though there are only a few research studies devoted to the comparison of Western and Russian adolescents, they seem to be coherent in the received results. Based on the data from Youth Self-Report (YSR), Child Behaviour Checklist (CBCL) and the Teacher's Report Form (TRF), Russian adolescents were lower on competencies and higher on somatic complaints and self-reported behavioural problems in comparison with an American sample (Slobodskaya, 1999). In the research devoted to the comparison of self-reported depressive symptoms between Russian and British schoolchildren (Child Depression Inventory [CDI] and Depression Self-Rating Scale [DSRS] were used), Russian pupils scored significantly higher on both scales (Charman & Pervova, 1996). A comparative study of Estonian and Russian schoolchildren also showed that Russian students experience higher levels of distress than Estonians (Andersson, 1997).

All the above-mentioned results lead us to expect the level of emotional distress and depressive symptoms in the Russian sample to be higher than in the Dutch one.

Motivation

The important role of motivation in the learning process was shown by research: academically motivated students (those who feel efficient and value learning) are more likely to be actively engaged in the educational process and to show better academic performance (Roeser et al, 1996, 1998a, 1998b).

International studies have documented that children in industrialised countries of eastern Europe and South-east Asia consistently outperform their peers in the United Kingdom and the USA, at least in science and mathematics (see Elliott et al, 1999). According to comparative research data, students in some Russian schools are significantly more motivated to learn than in some American and United

Kingdom schools: Russian students tend to be well motivated to attend class, undertake substantial out-of-school homework and value education in general (Elliott et al, 1999).

In the study by Hufton & Elliott (2000), a relatively high motivation of Russian schoolchildren was viewed as being attributed to school-related factors. It is suggested that the Russian school system creates the so-called 'pedagogical nexus', which is described as a set of linked, mutually reinforcing influences on pupils' motivational beliefs. Such a pedagogical nexus is 'institutionalised' in the schooling process and includes continuity of school, class and teacher; intergenerational continuity; specific mode of home-school relationships; the national curriculum and its manifestation in classroom pedagogy and textbooks; lesson organisation and assessment; the role of memorisation in learning, and others. All these elements seem to contribute to the motivation to learn and in general increase school achievement (see Hufton & Elliott, 2000).

Assuming that Dutch adolescents are being brought up and educated in the culture which can be defined as 'Western' and thus could exhibit similar patterns of academic motivation, we would expect academic motivation in Russian adolescents to be higher than in Dutch students of the same age.

Emotional Distress and Motivation

In this chapter, we investigate the ways in which emotional distress impacts on motivational beliefs. Recent research has documented that emotional distress in early adolescents has a negative influence on their motivational beliefs: pupils with internalising and externalising problems tend to feel academically incompetent and inefficient (Roeser et al, 1998a; Roeser, 1999). Nevertheless, the longitudinal study by Roeser et al (1998a) of American early adolescents found no significant correlation between emotional distress and academic value over a period of 2 years.

So, in this research, we test the hypothesis that emotional distress impacts negatively on academic motivation (self-efficacy and value beliefs) and can be viewed as a predictor of diminished motivation to learn for both Russian and Dutch early adolescents. Taking into consideration the research data that documented higher levels of both emotional distress and academic motivation in Russian students in comparison with their Western peers, we would expect to find different patterns of impact of emotional distress on academic motivation in Russian and Dutch early adolescents.

Research Instruments

Dutch Sample

The Dutch data used in this chapter were collected in March 2000 in the framework of two sets of research practice for third-year students of the University of Amsterdam (Huls et al, 2000; Van der Velden et al, 2000).

Participants. The first sample (Van der Velden et al, 2000) consisted of 288 adolescents (the number of girls and boys is unknown) from two different schools (a rural one and one in the city centre). All students attend classes in the first three grades of secondary education (12-15 years old). Both schools have a high percentage of students with Dutch ethnic background (98.4% for the rural school and 84.4% for the school in the city centre).

The second sample (Huls et al, 2000) consisted of 207 adolescents (103 boys and 104 girls) from two different schools; one in Heerhugowaard and another in Sittard. Both schools are schools for higher secondary education (HAVO and VWO). Pupils came from middle- and higher-class families. The data were collected in eight classrooms of these schools (four in each school). Some 93.7% of the participants have Dutch ethnic background.

Procedure. The questionnaires were translated from English into Dutch by a group of researchers in 1999.

Participants from the first sample filled in the questionnaires. No information was provided on whether they had received help from a teacher and/or a research assistant. The questionnaires from the second sample were filled in by the students in the classrooms. The pupils read and filled in the questionnaires by themselves. They were allowed to ask a teacher or a research assistant for help if they had any problems. Out of these two samples, 200 participants were randomly selected to form the Dutch sample used for the research.

Russian Sample

The data were collected in the city of Perm, situated at a distance of about 1300 kilometres to the east from Moscow. Perm, with a 1.3 million population, is one of the largest cities in the Urals and is an administrative, industrial and cultural centre of the Perm region.

Participants. The sample consisted of 175 adolescents: 76 boys (43%) and 99 girls (57%) from three different schools (N102, N25, N22). Schools 102 and 25 are regular schools, and school 22 is a school with specialist study of French and humanities, which means that the pupils go through a selective procedure when entering the institution. The pupils participating in the study were from one of the seventh and one of the eighth forms in each school. Data about the socio-economic status of the family were not available. The pupils were not asked about their ethnic background because the ethnic population in the city is more or less homogeneous and therefore ethnic questions in Perm are not as important as in some parts of the Netherlands and do not seem to be an influential factor that could have had an impact on the outcomes of the research. The youngest adolescent was 11.8 years old and the oldest was 14.8 years old. The mean age was 13.4 years.

Procedure. The questionnaires were translated from English into Russian by the group of researchers performing the survey, with the participation of a qualified interpreter. The translation was compared with the Dutch variant of the questionnaire. The questionnaires were accompanied by letters in Russian (for school heads, for classroom tutors and for the student him/herself). In these letters, the aim and procedure of the research were thoroughly explained. The questionnaires were then sent to the address of the Perm State Pedagogical University and were distributed among the schools randomly chosen by the University.

The questionnaires were filled in by the students in their classrooms. If the students had any difficulties, they were allowed to ask their teacher for help. The questionnaire forms were anonymous. In order to ensure confidentiality of responses, each student was provided with an envelope. After filling in the questionnaires, the students put them into the envelopes, and then sealed the envelopes. The completed questionnaires were collected from schools and sent back to the University of Amsterdam.

Measures

Motivation Measures

In order to assess academic motivation, Self-efficacy and Academic Value measures were used. Items were measured on a 5-point Likert scale (1 = not at all true of me to 5 = very true of me). The Self-efficacy scale (a = 0.71 [Russian sample]; a = 0.60 [Dutch sample]) was taken from the work of Midgley & Urdan (1995), and consisted of five items concerning students' perceived ability to master the material taught in their classrooms. The Academic Value scale (a = 0.75 [Russian sample]; a = 0.71 [Dutch sample]) consisted of four items that assessed students' perceived usefulness of the subject matter. These items were based on the work of Eccles (1983).

Emotional Distress Measures

In order to assess psychological well-being, several indicators of emotional distress were applied. One measure of emotional distress consisted of 36 items taken from Achenbach's (1991) Child Behavior Check List (a= 0.83 [Russian sample]; a= 0.89 [Dutch sample]). A 3-point scale was used for students' responses (0 = never, 1 = sometimes, 2 = often). These items assessed adolescents' self-reported symptoms of depression, anxiety, aggression, and anti-social behaviour during the 6 months prior to the research.

A measure of symptoms associated with depressed mood in the prior 2 weeks, that is the short form of Kovacs' (1992) Child Depression Inventory (a= 0.76 [Russian sample]; a = 0.74 [Dutch sample]) was also used. Students put a mark in the box next to one of three descriptions that they felt was an appropriate description of their feelings (e.g. 'I'm sad once in a while'; 'I'm sad many times; 'I am sad all the time').

A measure of test anxiety (a = 0.80 [Russian sample]; a = 0.87 [Dutch sample]) taken from the work by Pintrich & De Groot (1990) investigated students' concerns about their performance on classroom tests. Students had to respond to the items on a 5-point Likert scale (1 = not very true of me, to 5 = very true of me).

Results

Motivation in Dutch and Russian Adolescents

The mean and standard deviations on the Self-efficacy and Academic Value scales for Russian and Dutch samples are shown in Table I. The data were analysed by *t*-test with 'country' as a factor variable.

	Russia			The Netherlands		
	SD	n	Mean	SD	n	Mean
Self-efficacy	.5240	175	3.5794	.6042	193	3.5991
Academic Value	.5766	169	3.7181	.6371	195	3.6263

Table I. The mean and standard deviations on the Self-efficacy Land Academic Value scales for Russian and Dutch samples.

In contrast to our expectations, there are no significant differences between Russian and Dutch adolescents on either Self-efficacy or Academic Value scales.

Emotional Distress in Dutch and Russian Adolescents

The mean and standard deviations on the CBCL, CDI and Test Anxiety scales are shown in Table II. The data were analysed by *t*-test with 'country' as a factor variable.

In accordance with our expectations, Russian early adolescents scored significantly higher on all the above-mentioned scales: CBCL (internalising) scale (t [369] = -5.95, p <0. 001); CBCL (externalising) scale (t [369] = -5.25, p <0.001); CBCL (total) scale (t [369] = -6.74, p <0.001); CDI scale (t [369] = -6.08, p <0.001); Test Anxiety scale (t [369] = -5.51, p <0.001).

	Russia			The Netherlands		
	SD	n	Mean	SD	n	Mean
CBCL (internalising)	.3048	175	.5616	.3206	196	.3683
CBCL (externalising)	.2779	175	.5419	.2510	196	.3971
CBCL (total)	.2485	175	.5504	.2232	196	.3844
CDI	.2502	175	.4452	.3006	196	.2712
Test Anxiety	.8955	175	3.0577	.8615	196	2.5539

Table II. The mean and standard deviations on the CBCL, CDI and Test Anxiety scales.

Discriminant analysis. By means of discriminant analysis, we tested the degree of difference on both Emotional Distress and Academic Value scales between Dutch and Russian samples. The fact that 74.5% of Dutch and 66.3% of Russian adolescents were correctly classified proves that there are significant differences between these two samples.

Discriminant analysis supported the results of the *t*-Test analysis. Discriminant function coefficients documented significant differences between Dutch and Russian samples on Emotional Distress scales: CDI (0.72), CBCL (internalising) (0.71), test anxiety (0.65) and CBCL (externalising) (0.62). Discriminant function coefficients of Academic Value and Self-efficacy scales showed no significant differences between the samples.

Relations between Indicators of Emotional Distress and Motivation

In order to examine the impact of emotional distress on academic motivation in Russian and Dutch early adolescents, we employed regression analysis technique with Emotional Distress scales as independent and Self-efficacy and Academic Value scales as dependent variables.

Regression analysis showed that emotional distress was not a significant predictor of diminished self-efficacy in the Dutch sample. In the Russian sample, test anxiety (= -0.37, t [175] = -5.04, p <0.001), CDI (= -0.19, t [175] = -2.12, p <0.05), and CBCL (externalising) (= -0.26,

t [175] = -3.67, p <0.001) are significant predictors of diminished self-efficacy, and CBCL (internalising) (= 0.24, t [175] = 2.65, p <0.01) is a significant predictor of enhanced self-efficacy beliefs.

The CBCL (externalising) scale was a significant predictor of diminished academic value both in the Dutch sample (= -0.26, t [175] = -.67, p <0.001] and Russian (=-0.32, t [175] = -4.18, p <0.001) samples.

In accordance with our expectations, the influence of emotional distress on academic motivation acquires different patterns in Russian and Dutch adolescents. The influence of distress (externalising problems) on value beliefs was detrimental for academic value beliefs in both samples. The major differences were found in the way emotional distress influences self-efficacy beliefs. If in the Dutch sample, emotional distress was not a significant predictor of diminished efficacy beliefs, in the Russian sample, depressive symptoms, externalising problems and signs of test anxiety were significant predictors of diminished self-efficacy beliefs, and internalising problems were even positively correlated with self-efficacy.

Discussion

In this study, we examined the differences in the levels of emotional distress and academic motivation of Russian and Dutch early adolescents as well as the patterns of the impact emotional distress has on academic value and self-efficacy beliefs.

Emotional Distress

In accordance with our expectations, Russian early adolescents scored significantly higher on all Emotional Distress scales: CBCL total, CBCL internalising, CBCL externalising, CDI and test anxiety scales.

One of the possible explanations of higher level of emotional distress and behavioural problems displayed by Russian students is an unfavourable socio-economic situation in contemporary Russia. The relation of unfavourable socio-economic factors and signs of problem behaviour and depressive symptoms in children and adolescents is still a matter for further research. Nevertheless, we suppose that social and economic turmoil can have a negative impact on early adolescents' psychological well-being via different pathways (family: parental unemployment and impoverishment, parental feelings of uncertainty, decrease of adult authority and control [see Slobodskaya, 1999]; school: decrease of resources and financial support and hence perceived changes in teachers' attitudes; community: breach of school-community relationships; general culture shift).

Other possible explanations for the findings could lie in the differences of the school psychological environments in Russia and the

Netherlands. School psychological environment research deals with the meanings individuals derive from their experiences in a certain learning setting, and thus aims at studying students' perceptions of school practices (Maehr & Midgely, 1991; Roeser et al, 1998a). One of the major components of perceived school environment is achievement goal structure, understood in terms of certain patterns of learning and behaviour that lead to success and in the long run influence students' psychological well-being and school outcomes (Maehr et al, 1991; Kaplan & Maehr, 1999). Research has documented that different achievement goal structures can be emphasised in different school settings. The major division is made between task goal and ability goal structures. Task goal structure is concentrated on effort and personal improvement as hallmarks of competence. It reinforces understanding and skill acquisition. Task mastery and students' involvement regardless of the level of their present ability are being acknowledged. School settings acquiring this type of goal structures can be characterised by recognition of academic improvement and progress, non-competitive academic requirements and project-based learning (Maehr et al, 1991; Roeser et al, 1998a). Ability goal structure, on the contrary, is characterised as supporting competitiveness and social comparison in learning situations. Schools with this kind of goal structure tend to treat higher grades attainment as the most important goal of learning and introduce more favourable treatment to the highest achieving students by means of all-school award ceremonies, special privileges and enhanced educational opportunities for higher attaining students. Outperforming others in such a school setting is encouraged (Maehr et al, 1991).

Research has documented that students in schools emphasising ability structures tend to exhibit more problems and less positive views of self. In the long run, perception of school as concentrating on ability goals may undermine engagement with school (Roeser et al, 1996), have a negative effect on general psychological well-being of students, and result in feelings of frustration, disaffection and self-consciousness (Kaplan et al, 1999).

As mentioned by Kondratiev (1997), the traditional Russian school is organised in such a way that failures of one category of students create a favourable background for the success of others. Applying the concept of two different achievement goal structures explained above, we suggest that an ability goal structure is predominant in Russian schools and can add to the pressures Russian early adolescents experience on this developmental stage and result in higher levels of emotional distress in Russian students.

We suppose that school context can also influence the self-concept of Russian early adolescents. It has been documented that children in Russia are subjected to strong pressure at school (Andersson, 1997). Teachers do not praise students enough for their work and use a lot of criticism, which does not contribute to the formation of a positive self-image (Slobodskaya, 1999).

Higher distress demonstrated by Russian participants could also be attributed to the time the Russian data were collected. Students filled in the questionnaires in March, which is the end of the third academic term, perceived as the most important one in the academic year. So, we suppose that students could have been more tense and stressed at that period.

Academic Motivation

In contrast to our expectations, no significant differences in academic motivation between Russian and Dutch students were found.

There could be several explanations for that. Firstly, our expectations were based on the assumption that Dutch students brought up and educated in Western society would show similar levels of academic motivation to adolescents in other Western countries (the UK and USA). The results suggest that there are differences in academic motivation between adolescents in Western countries and they should be taken into consideration. It is also important to note that results received in comparative research based on data retrieval in specific geographical areas are not representative of particular nations or whole cultures and should be treated with caution (see Elliott et al, 1999).

Secondly, motivation as a widespread term can be understood differently, depending on the researcher's background and/or methodology employed. There are certain differences in the ways academic motivation was conceptualised in the previous research and in our study. In the studies by Elliott et al (1999) and Hufton & Elliott (2000), which served as a basis for our expectations, motivation was understood in terms of students' performance levels. In the Elliott et al study (1999), students' perceptions and satisfaction with their current levels of performance and work rate (class attendance, homework completion and other) and value of education as an end in itself or as a means for a desirable economic or vocational future were examined. Our research conceptualised motivation as consisting of value and self-efficacy beliefs, and thus was mostly concerned with adolescents' views of self and their valuing of current academic activities. This could add to the differences found in our research and in the previous research, as well as the fact that the participants of the above-mentioned study were middle adolescents (14-15 years old).

Though no significant differences in academic value and self-efficacy beliefs were found, we suppose that the sources of these beliefs could be different. Earlier research has documented that adolescents in some United Kingdom and American schools exhibit higher levels of satisfaction with the levels of their academic achievement and work rate.

Russian students of the same age have more negative perceptions of their performance and tend to mention that they do not work as hard as they could. It is suggested that teachers in the United Kingdom and USA place more positive construction on students' work. This leads to the Western tendency to encourage high self-esteem regardless of high performance. Among Russian teachers, on the contrary, critical attitude to performance is widespread: they tend to point out what is wrong in a piece of work rather than what is good (see Elliott et al, 1999). Thus, self-efficacy in Dutch adolescents could be formed by a more positive construction of achievement by teachers. In Russian students, self-efficacy beliefs could be developed in the course of overcoming hardships in the atmosphere of competitiveness and school pressure. There was no control for achievement levels in this study so we do not have solid evidence for these presuppositions.

Some qualitative differences in value could be mentioned. American and United Kingdom adolescents are supposed to exhibit instrumental value beliefs (education as a means for good employment and economic prosperity), while Russians value education as an end in itself (to be literate and cultured has been traditionally valued in Russian society) (see Elliott et al, 1999). Further research involving qualitative methodology to unveil the sources of self-efficacy and value beliefs is needed.

Emotional Distress and Its Impact on Academic Motivation

As we expected, different patterns were found of the impact of emotional distress on academic motivation in the Russian and Dutch samples.

Our results partly confirm the results of Roeser et al (1998a), which documented no significant correlation between emotional distress and academic value in a sample of American adolescents over a period of 2 years. Nevertheless, we found externalising problems in both Russian and Dutch students to be a significant predictor for diminished academic value beliefs. And unsurprisingly, active opposition to school regulations seems to be a sign of decreased value of school-related activities.

Major differences between the samples were found in the way emotional distress influences self-efficacy beliefs. If in the Dutch sample emotional distress was not a significant predictor of diminished efficacy beliefs, in the Russian sample, depressive symptoms, externalising problems and signs of test anxiety were significant predictors of diminished self-efficacy beliefs, and (quite a striking result) internalising problems were even positively correlated with self-efficacy.

The possible explanations for the findings are as follows. The differences in the emotional distress levels could be an explanation of the fact that externalising problems, depressive symptoms and test anxiety serve as significant predictors of diminished self-efficacy beliefs among Russian early adolescents. We did not measure threshold levels of emotional distress for Russian and Dutch students. The presence of high distress could explain its significant influence on self-efficacy beliefs among Russian adolescents and absence of the significant influence of this variable in the Dutch sample.

The fact that internalising problems serve as positive predictors for self-efficacy beliefs seems puzzling at first. Probably, by means of internalising problems, Russian adolescents cope with the different pressures they face. According to Bandura (1997), a resilient sense of efficacy requires experience in overcoming obstacles through effort, as difficulties provide the necessary opportunities to learn how to turn failure into success. The need for self-regulation and control as important constituents of self-efficacy beliefs could lead to the internalisation of the existing problems in the atmosphere of a wide range of pressures when one has to rely on oneself as an important resource for problem-solving. School could also contribute to such a kind of relation. Students tend to perceive certain pathways leading to success, and as academic involvement is understood in terms of being concerned and even worried, it is possible to suggest the sense of efficacy is linked with constant self-appraisal and self-mastery.

Limitations and Conclusion

Several limitations are important to note regarding the study. First, there was no control for gender in this study. It is believed that there are significant differences in the types of problems exhibited by boys and girls in adolescence. That is why it would be interesting to compare gender differences in Russian and Dutch adolescents.

Second, in this study, we examined only a one-way relation between emotional distress and academic motivation. At the same time, it is possible to suggest that the relation is more complex than that. Earlier research has documented that adolescents' perception of academic competence could be a an important personal resource that contributes to the feelings of esteem, and academic value not only indicates positive school adjustment modes among students, but also gives a sense of direction and purpose that can protect adolescents against feelings of distress and involvement in problem behaviour (see Roeser et al, 1998a). Thus, it could be expected that the relations between academic and emotional functioning are reciprocal over time, and further research is needed to track down these relations.

Third, the research tools used in this study are widely spread in Western research practices and are new to Russian psychological and educational research. As Charman & Pervova (1996) warn, the differences in cultural and language interpretations of the terms used in the questionnaires could influence the results obtained, and while performing further research, the technique of independent back-translation is needed.

In conclusion, we aimed to explore the differences in the levels of emotional distress and academic motivation in Dutch and Russian early adolescence and unveil the ways emotional distress impacts academic motivation. The results suggest that there are considerable differences in the emotional distress domain and in patterns of emotional distress impact on motivational beliefs between Dutch and Russian samples. We suppose that further comparative research could add to the knowledge about the sources of stress and problem behaviour in adolescents and help shape educational practices and social services to match the needs individuals have during this developmental period.

Acknowledgements

We would like to thank Professor Dr J.C. van der Wolf for his help and illuminating discussions we had while working on this chapter. We also want to thank the Vice-Rector for Science and Foreign Relations of Perm State Pedagogical University, Dr A.K. Kolesnikov, for his assistance in the course of this research. We are indebted to Prof. John Sayer from the University of Oxford for reading the manuscript and for his important remarks. We are very grateful to school heads, teachers and, of course, students for making it all possible.

References

Achenbach, T.M. (1991) *Integrative Guide for the 1991 CBCL/4-18 YSR, and TRF Profiles.* Burlington: University of Vermont, Department of Psychiatry.

Andersson, E. (1997) Pupils' Experiences of School and Family Life. A Comparison between Estonia and Russia, *Social Behavior and Personality*, 25, pp. 201-210.

Bandura, A. (1997) *Self-efficacy: the exercise of control.* New York: W.H. Freeman.

Boekaerts, M. (1993) Being Concerned with Well-being and with Learning, *Educational Psychologist*, 28, pp. 149-167.

Borman, K. & Schneider, B. (Eds) (1998) *The Adolescent Years: social influences and educational challenges.* Chicago: University of Chicago Press.

Brannen, J., Dodd, K., Oakley, A. & Storey, P. (1994) *Young People, Health and Family Life.* Buckingham: Open University Press.

Charman, T. & Pervova, I. (1996) Self-Reported Depressed Mood in Russian and UK Schoolchildren. A Research Note, *Journal of Child Psychology and Psychiatry*, 37, pp. 879-883.

Crijnen, A.A.M., Achenbach, T.M. & Verhulst, F.C. (1997) Comparison of Problems Reported by Parents of Children in 12 Cultures: total problems, externalizing, and internalising, *Journal of American Academy of Child and Adolescent Psychiatry*, 36, pp. 1269-1277.

Eccles, J. (1983) Expectancies, Values and Academic Behaviours, in J.T. Spence (Ed.) *The Development of Achievement* Motivation, pp. 283-331. Greenwich, CT: JAI.

Elliott, J., Hufton, N., Hildreth, A. & Illushin, L. (1999) Factors Influencing Educational Motivation: a study of attitudes, expectations and behaviour of children in Sunderland, Kentucky and St Petersburg, *British Educational Research Journal*, 25, pp. 75-94.

Evans, P. (1995) Children and Youth at Risk, in Organisation for Economic Cooperation and Development *Our Children at Risk*, pp. 13-50. Paris: Organisation for Economic Cooperation and Development.

Hufton, N. & Elliott, J. (2000) Motivation to Learn: the pedagogical nexus in the Russian school: some implications for transnational research and policy borrowing, *Educational Studies*, 26, pp. 115-136.

Huls, M., Spanjaard, S., Boersma, I. & Mortier, S. de M. (2000) *Hoe hangt geexternaliseerd en geintrenaliseerd probleemgedrag samen met sekse en hoe komt dit tot uiting in de waardering voor de school en de doelmatigheid van de leerlingen?* unpublished research paper, University of Amsterdam.

Kaplan, A. & Maehr, M.L. (1999) Achievement Goals and Student Well-being, *Contemporary Educational Psychology*, 24, pp. 330-358.

Kondratiev, M.U. (1997) *Tipichnie deviatsii psikhosocialnogo razvitia podrostkov* (Typical deviations in psychosocial development of adolescents), in *Podrostok v zamknutom kruge obshenia* (Adolescent in an exclusive circle of communication), pp. 24-39. Moscow.

Kovacs, M. (1992) *Children's Depression Inventory Manual*. North Tonawada, NY: Multi-Health Systems, Inc.

Maehr, M.L. & Midgely, C. (1991) Enhancing Student Motivation: a schoolwide approach, *Educational Psychologist*, 26, pp. 399-427.

McMahon, R.J. & Peters, R. DeV. (Eds) (1990) *Behavior Disorders of Adolescence. Research, Intervention and Policy in Clinical and School Settings*. New York: Plenum.

Midgley, C. & Urdan, T. (1995) Predictors of Middle School Students' Use of Self-handicapping Strategies, *Journal of Early Adolescence*, 15, pp. 389-412.

Pintrich P.R. & De Groot, E. (1990) Motivation and Self-regulated Learning Components of Classroom Academic Performance, *Journal of Educational Psychology*, 82, pp. 33-40.

Roeser, R.W., Eccles, J.S. & Sameroff, A.J. (1998a) Academic and Emotional Functioning in Early Adolescence: longitudinal relations, patterns, and prediction by experience in middle school, *Development and Psychopathology*, 10, pp. 321-352.

Roeser, R.W., Eccles, J.S. & Strobel, K.R. (1998b) Linking the Study of Schooling and Mental Health: selected issues and empirical illustrations at the level of the individual, *Educational Psychologist*, 33, pp. 153-176.

Roeser, R.W., Midgley, C. & Urdan, T.C. (1996) Perceptions of the School Psychological Environment and Early Adolescents' Psychological and

Behavioral Functioning in School: the mediating role of goals and belonging, *Journal of Educational Psychology*, 88, pp. 408-422.

Roeser, R.W. (1999) Assessing Patterns of Motivation and Mental Health among Early Adolescents, unpublished research paper, Stanford University.

Rutter, M. & Rutter, M. (1992) *Developing Minds: challenge and continuity across the life span*. London, Penguin.

Slobodskaya, H.R. (1999) Competence, Emotional and Behavioural Problems in Russian Adolescents, *European Child and Adolescent Psychiatry*, 8, pp. 173-180.

Swanson, D.N., Spencer, M.B. & Petersen, A. (1998) Identity Formation in Adolescence, in K. Borman & B. Schneider (Eds) *The Adolescent Years: social influences and educational challenges*, pp. 18-41. Chicago: University of Chicago Press.

Tsukerman, G.A. (1998) 10-12-letnie: 'Nichya zemlia' v vozrastnoi psikhologii (10-12-year-olds: 'no man's land' in developmental psychology), *Voprosy Psikhologii*, 3, pp. 17-31.

Van der Velden, A., Murphy, J.M., Rourou, A. & Lanting, H. (2000) Verslag onderzoekspracticum, Unpublished research paper, University of Amsterdam.

Preparing Teachers for Health Education in Schools: the new TEMPUS project in Perm

ALASTAIR WHITE

The Background to Health Priorities in Perm and Russia

TEMPUS-TACIS Joint European Project 10830 grew out of its predecessor, exploiting the existing infrastructure of contacts, expertise and working patterns to address an issue which had become an evident and growing problem in the district of Perm. In the course of the previous project addressing special needs, it became apparent that alongside the learning difficulties of many children within the school system, there were pressing issues of poor health: a seriously polluted environment, economic problems, and increasing social difficulties have all contributed to the worsening health of the population and of young people in particular.

In 1997/78, 85% of children suffered from allergies of different kinds; 67% were held to suffer from mental or behavioural difficulties; in the same year among children in the Perm region, the one-year increase in heart problems was 2.5%; stomach problems increased by 1.6%; motor difficulties increased by 2.4%; and inborn diseases increased by 1.7%. Half the children within the school system were identified as retarded. These local figures in themselves are grave cause for concern.

However, the wider picture in Russia as a whole is also alarming, particularly in the growth of health problems which reflect social factors, and which predominantly afflict young people – specifically, sexually transmitted diseases, intravenous drug use, and incidence of HIV infection. By way of example, the World Heath Organisation (WHO) reported in early 1998 that the number of notified cases of syphilis in Russia as a whole had risen from 6000 in 1988 to 390,000 in 1996, a 62-fold increase, and representing a figure of 170 infected people per

100,000 of population. Other figures place it higher; it compares with a figure of about 5 per 100,000 in the countries of northern and western Europe.

Drug abuse is also an ever-increasing problem at a national level. Moscow is said by the WHO to have an intravenous drug-using population of 100,000. Dr Karl Dehne, representing UNAIDS at a conference in 1997, maintained that there were half a million intravenous drug users in Russia at that time. Linked to the increase in drug use and the increase in sexually transmitted disease is, of course, the fact of an explosion in HIV infection. Starting from 1995, in which there were less than 200 new reported cases of HIV infection in the Russian Federation, and well under 2000 overall, it is the view of the Russian Ministry of Health that there were likely to be 800,000 people in Russia who were HIV positive by the end of the year 2000. More recent views suggest that this may have been an underestimate.

There are, then, grave problems: these are likely to be exacerbated by the fact that people suffering from the symptoms of sexually transmitted disease are between 50 and 300 times more likely to contract HIV from sexual contact with someone who is positive. The context of this growing problem is bleak, then: there is liberalisation in Russia, but Russia has not yet developed fully coherent approaches to sex and drugs education; there is a huge increase in afflictions such as sexually transmitted diseases and drug abuse, and yet there are declining health budgets.

These issues are, as I have said, national ones. Perm, however, is no more of an island than anywhere else, and is inevitably to be affected by the picture in the rest of the Russian Federation. Perm, then, faces the twin issues of addressing the local situation, with the chronic health difficulties associated with a legacy of environmental and economic degradation, as well as anticipating these looming national problems.

The Context for the New Project: Perm State
Pedagogical University and international collaboration

The prime stated objective of the JEP is to help the Perm State Pedagogical University develop its capability to help provide a continuum of teacher training for health education in the Perm region. The understanding established over the course of the previous JEP dictated that the project should continue to build on the collaborative efforts of University, schools, city, and region to extend the work of the JEP partner group into a self-sustaining approach to health education. The first year of the project has successfully sought to maintain and strengthen the institutional self-development that characterised the success of the first project: the most telling evidence of this lies in the growing reputation of TEMPUS in the region, the readiness and enthusiasm with which trainers and students are embarking on the new courses, and the willingness of the University to restructure timetables and accommodation to embrace the logistical needs of the new course, including the involvement of training staff drawn from a wide range of university faculties.

Perm State Pedagogical University, which prepares the majority of teachers serving a region of 3 million people, has already established a 1-year course promoting strategies for inclusive school approaches to children with SEN.

It has already established working partnerships with pilot schools, and established an increasingly well-equipped university-based resource centre. There is, for example, the potential to use existing ICT facilities to provide access to health care programmes, resources, and methodology to each of the 50 districts of the Perm region.

The success of the last project and the progressive thinking of those in Perm means that the key teams in the city public services, the medical community, and the education service are working in concert to promote health awareness. A measure of this coherence of thinking lies in the enthusiasm with which the new city administration accommodated the new project into their thinking, in the first months of the new administration in 2001.

The University has a record of interdisciplinary, inter-faculty creation of new courses, and has (through the Departments of Pedagogy and Social Work and the Department of Anatomy and Physiology) an existing health care knowledge base. This knowledge base can be used to extend professional development through in-service training, the 1-year course for selected professionals from the school system: this course will generate increasing numbers of trained key teaching staff, who will themselves act as agents of change both within schools and, through in-service dissemination, across schools. Short courses will enhance the readiness of other school-based colleagues to take a role in the dissemination of good practice at school level.

Furthermore, in the continued partnership with the Universities of Halle, Amsterdam and Oxford, there exist many opportunities for the sharing of other models for dealing with health issues: partners in the consortium can contribute school-based health education models for different age ranges, multifaceted expertise in child health through links with other agencies, wide experience of family-school links, initiatives in teacher training, and our own experiences of developing inclusive educational policies within our own local or national systems. In addition, the people involved in these challenges in the partner countries have, for the most part, considerable understanding of the situation in Perm through their involvement in the previous project, as well as the loyalty and commitment that comes through that contact.

A crucial factor in the success of the new project lies in the extent to which the health education curriculum is felt (by the teacher students on the in-service courses) to be relevant to their needs in school, adaptable within the curricular and management structures of their schools, and transferable to the classroom. The planned curriculum seeks to balance physiological awareness with understanding of new educational technologies, approaches to school leadership and the management of change in relation to health education, the management of and provision for children with physical or psychological difficulties, understanding of narcotics, education relating to the body, and 'education for a healthy way of life'.

As I write, the first year of the PSPU taught course moves into its final third, and the extent to which evaluation of this first year is able to generate curriculum amendments is very important. There is much to be done – the first run of the course will have provided important indicators about the right methodological and curriculum balance for the future, and the work done in the pilot schools will clarify further the nature of the health issues and the in-service needs of teachers and school leaders. The extent to which the work of the University in Perm is able to be disseminated effectively to teachers and children, and the sustainability of that dissemination, are surely key measures of continued success.

Study visits to Halle, Amsterdam and Oxford have all, it is to be hoped, contributed in their own ways to the continued evaluation and evolution of practice in Perm. In the first year of the course, study visitors from the Perm team between them visited government agencies dedicated to health promotion, health care centres, centres for drugs education, foundations for research into sexually transmitted diseases and centres for drug addiction treatment, and talked to those who have set up physical exercise programmes for children with physical disabilities, those who work with drug dependent families, community dieticians and school nutritionists, and many others. Of course, they have also visited many types of schools, looking at health education in all its many forms, and at models of sensitive curricular provision for those children who in another era would not have had the chance to be educated inclusively.

In discussion with the course leaders in Perm, returned from their study visits to the different partner countries of the EU, it was clear that what was most remarkable was the convergence and correlation of core principles espoused by different institutions in different countries: wherever you start from, all seem broadly in agreement on the central priorities, objectives, and methodologies that inform effective health education at the moment, encapsulated in this model offered by our consultant from the Netherlands: health education priorities – to improve health and life expectancy; to avoid early death; and to improve quality of life – in other words, a policy designed to anticipate and preempt problems, rather than one that finds itself always reacting to disease and ill health. Without claiming to be all-inclusive, the lists that follow offer a full enough description of the content and methodology of much of the successful work we have encountered in the course of the project so far.

Key Health Education Issues

Sex education
Drugs education
Food and nutrition
Smoking
Alcohol
Hygiene routines
Families
Relationships
Puberty and adolescence
Exercise

This list is striking in its non-medical, non-technical character, and in the importance it attaches to social and interpersonal aspects of development, seeing them as integral to the healthy development of the individual. The next noteworthy aspect of the shared thinking of the EU partners in their current approaches to health education in schools lies in the methodology and delivery of school-based health education programmes; again, there is a high incidence of shared thinking.

How to Present Issues in Schools

Need for language that children and teachers can share
Need for study of health issues to be active
Need for children to create their own reactions
Need to inform, not instruct
Giving children time/space/freedom to learn
Need to allow children to learn by making their own decisions

Again, there are powerful pointers here: it is clear that traditional approaches, epitomised perhaps by the Nancy Reagan 'Just say no' anti-drugs campaign, and further characterised by a presumption of superior knowledge (and the right to prescribe 'wisdom' on the part of the teacher), are not seen as effective ways of encouraging healthy attitudes amongst schoolchildren. On the contrary, there is a profound emphasis on ensuring that the language, experience, and outcomes of the health education curriculum should all operate at the level of the child, at whatever age; that children should understand, think, involve themselves in discussion, and decide for themselves, based on accessible information.

Beyond these, there are further areas of strong convergence of thinking, all of which now play a part in Perm's emergent health education approaches:

Need to start very young
Need to include families in health education
Need to keep parents involved and informed
Commitment of senior management, working with a nominated teacher-leader
Importance of in-service training
Allocation of secure weekly curriculum time, and occasional extended intensive time
Need for health messages to be supported across the curriculum
Support for the health education message in the wider school/community environment
Evolution of healthy eating school catering
Need to integrate children with disabilities
Need to prioritise personal well-being of troubled children above the subject curriculum – this linked to the importance of school counsellors
Need for teachers to know medical information about individuals
Involvement of multiple agencies (health/community/social services) to use expertise to prepare resources/presentations; to use research; to inform health professionals about schools and students

These preoccupations and conclusions have, then, formed the backbone of the first exploratory year of the project. Constraints of time and the need to initiate courses have meant that the first year's courses pre-date much of the findings of this period, and the process of evaluation and review will be critical in introducing changes for next year. Increasingly, course leaders in Perm are talking of the need to rethink methodological as well as pedagogical approaches, persuaded, perhaps, of the precept that without appropriate classroom practice, curriculum content scarcely matters. In this respect, a welcome legacy of the last project lies in the insistence that course members conduct part of their work through school-based investigation and practice. This will surely act as one effective measure of the usefulness of the course.

Moving towards More Effective Provision – PSPU and its partners

A priority of the project has been to promote support and sponsorship for the JEP: it is a strength of the project that much goodwill exists already, but the project has identified the need to involve a wider range of senior school-based professionals in the project, through a series of meetings in Perm. Groups of headteachers and senior school managers have met with health education professionals and headteachers from the West to discuss possibilities for local implementation, and, as mentioned before, the involvement of elected officials and senior civil servants at regional and city levels remains a huge bonus. Crucially, the project benefits from the commitment by the city and regional authorities to guarantee continued funding of teacher secondees and teacher trainer salaries for the university courses for a minimum of a further 4 years, looking well beyond the end date of the JEP funding itself. The support of city and region is further reflected in the qualifications and remuneration enhancement that is enjoyed by those who successfully complete the course.

The emphasis on dissemination, stronger now that we are into the second year of the project, depends on several tiers of support: those mentioned earlier, involving school-based and regional leaders; and the growing involvement of young teachers in initial teacher training, all of whom now study a module dedicated to health education. Beyond this, exposure to the new project has extended to others not directly involved, setting up meetings that describe project thinking to headteachers, senior managers, and public authority bodies from across the city and beyond. The purpose is to encourage more participative management practice, and to allow the thinking and learning of course members to be more readily accessible to school managers. There is, then, a virtuous circle of city and regional support, university commitment, school enthusiasm, and the status afforded by the publication of two books about the last project (in Russian and English) that continues to be built on in this project. While the nature and direction of the project is ultimately in the hands of the Joint Management Group, there is a sense of ownership, shared responsibility, and a long-term commitment to negotiated consortium leadership that augurs well.

The success of the project depends significantly on the growing capacity of the TEMPUS resources room at PSPU to offer a workspace, research materials, school resources, and electronic dissemination of international approaches to health education. Colleagues in partner countries have been instrumental in providing large quantities of published and project-generated materials relating to health education, for consideration by colleagues in Russia. These include purchased research publications, published school resources, home-made school resources, education authority publications, commercial and home-made video resources, and so on. These materials are assessed for adaptation for use on the course, and as support material for trainers and students; some are translated. Herein lies another area of potential development, with the opportunity to allocate more translation energy and resources to the creation of simply phrased, child-friendly, school-based materials, and perhaps less to the translation of university-level research documents.

There is a possibility that the work of the TEMPUS room may support the stated intention of the city authorities to use its funding and organisational powers to resource and disseminate support into the schools, through a programme of material and policy support for the wider in-school implementation of project thinking in terms of health education. Clearly, though, the single biggest source of materials, thinking, and information exchange is the Internet, and the steady growth of this as a tool in the work of course students and schools could have an enormous impact on access to health education ideas.

Main Aims for the Second Half of the Project

Given that the project enjoys high status, secure course funding beyond the cessation of EU money, the commitment of very able colleagues in Perm, and a growing resource base, then it becomes possible to look forward to the future with confidence. However, Perm has been memorably described as 'the region of evergreen tomatoes', and there are difficulties in Perm which the project will continue to face, one of which is wider funding for schools. Dr Tatiana Margolina, the Vice-Governor of Perm region, expressed the scale of this in a recent meeting. One in three schools in the region is in need of major and urgent repairs, there is a need for 26 new schools, and there are 2000 teaching vacancies in the Perm region alone. Teacher pay is extremely modest, about a third of a factory wage, and most teachers would need to supplement their salaries with other employment. In the city, there is a growing sense that teachers will need to have their housing costs subsidised.

Another key area is that of overcoming the legacy of many decades of pedagogical and methodological narrowness. At school and at university level, there is inevitably a residual trace of this, complicated by the lack of resources and the underfunding of the infrastructure of educational provision at both school and university levels. Colleagues in Russia have achieved remarkable things in the few years since liberalisation, and continue to do so, but time and money continue to be needed. One course leader spoke eloquently about this issue of pedagogical and methodological reform, seeking to identify it as, in his view, the central prerequisite of project success: he spoke of the need to take a complex approach, working through the culture of the whole school. He spoke, too, of needing to identify the main unit and agent of change as the lesson – 10,000 of them, over the years – the need to change so that the child is at the centre of the lesson, in aims, activities, collaboration and reflection. He stressed the need for a culture of questioning by students, aiding both intellectual and emotional motivation, and leading to 'self-sustaining' work. He identified learning through 'difficult success' as being central to improvements, without which health education would not improve. Another colleague spoke of the 'zone of proximate success', highlighting the importance of offering a curriculum provision which is simultaneously accessible and stretching to the students. These contributions articulate lucidly the movement from a scientific, hierarchical delivery of pedagogy towards one which is much more aware of the needs of the child in the school and the teacher in the classroom.

A key recent development in Perm, and one likely to be helpful to the project, lies in the elevation of Dr Tatiana Margolina to the Vice-Governorship of Perm Region. Dr Margolina has been very supportive of TEMPUS work in the past, and her new role holds promise for two key reasons: first, she is a formidable political presence with deep sympathies with a project that needs sustained political support, both during and beyond the period of EU funding; and second, her current role gives her an influence over the region as a whole, at a time when there is a need for the project to look towards the region more systematically, most of the emphasis so far having been in the city. It is worth recording here the detailed substance of our recent meeting with her. Dr Margolina expressed her commitment to the project, and spoke of:

> her sense of the importance of health education spreading region-wide;
>
> the importance of the political administration being seen to offer sustainable political support;
>
> the recognition that the objectives of the project have to be seen as long term and gradual; and she
>
> applauded the principle of school managers using PSPU-trained teachers as models of good practice, and those same teachers having a dissemination role beyond their own schools;
>
> talked of the desirability of establishing a needs-based health curriculum, by which I understood her to mean one that was based on actual community health needs, rather than an academic/extrinsic imposition of medical knowledge;
>
> spoke of the pressures that exist on the system as a whole – that financial support is available only to some of the poorest, that the school system faces a backlog of repairs that mean that many school buildings remain structurally dangerous.

The second part of the meeting was dedicated to her thinking for the future. It is no exaggeration to suggest that her ideas here may well form the single most powerful impetus to the next year or so of the course, and the project is fortunate indeed to have such an influential source of support. Dr Margolina went on to discuss:

> the setting up of regional financial support systems, offering holiday camps and physical exercise groups as models for communities, centrally funded. This channelling of resources from key funding sources has the potential, being based on needs-analysis, to provide a picture of the needs of the region;

the setting up of a Healthy Population working subgroup;
the need to recognise that no authority can be successful without the support of the people, and that no management system can deliver successful initiatives without working effectively with the people likely to be affected by those management systems.

The last part of our meeting with Tatiana Margolina related to perhaps the most promising development in Perm during the entire project. We are keen to use this development as a central building block in our strategic direction over the next 18 months. It relates to news that Dr Margolina had recently received from Moscow:

the crucial announcement that Moscow has delivered a federation-wide recommendation that the regions develop networks of health centres, specifically linked to schools, to promote community health; and that these centres develop interdisciplinary approaches to health problems, drawing on social services support, the health division, and sporting bodies, all within one financial framework.

This last piece of news seems most opportune. There is the potential here to use a Moscow-generated initiative (though it is not supported by funding) to initiate a series of school-based, community-linked health education centres, perhaps with staffing which places preventative and 'holistic' notions of health and health education above technical and medical expertise. Dr Margolina's enthusiasm for this was also echoed by two other influential colleagues, Dr Galina Gutnik and Viktor Gusarov, at the heart of the regional administration. The centres have the potential to act not only as accessible, low-cost, local drop-in centres, but also as centres of resources, both paper and technical, as well as sources of in-service support and training.

Project colleagues from Halle have been researching mechanisms and structures through which such a centre might become effective in the implementation and dissemination of good practice: they have worked in the area of changing school systems, changes which require a change in school culture, and involving the briefing of headteachers, establishing criteria for pilot school involvement, the integration of academic study with in-school implementation, the provision of continuing programmes of workshops for school leaders to help implementation, supervision of students, sharing and exchange of experience, the twin developments of personal and professional development alongside institutional development, and the need to build networks of good practice. This last is self-evident, and crucial. There is neither the need nor the resourcing to reinvent the wheel in each school, and this model of development could be seen as useful in the Perm context.

There is also the potential to coordinate pre-school and post-school health education through these centres. Dr Galina Gutnik, a key figure in the city administration, asserted the need to develop a health education culture all the way from the kindergarten to university level, with parents, teachers, and children all involved within a system in which teachers and health educators can model effective health education both in the school and to the wider community. The importance of the early years was further elucidated in another contribution, in which a course leader spoke of the importance of recognising the subjective experience of the world that the young child has, and the need to recognise both physical and social dimensions in the well-being of the child. Interestingly, there is a strong sense that that the physical well-being of the child is not predestined at this time, but is subject to 'change and choice' – through hygiene, exercise, sport, environment, illness prevention, and etiquette – and this represents a significant shift away from the defectology culture of the previous era. Perm no longer seeks to define health in terms of its opposite, illness. The colleague concerned spoke also of the psychological dimensions of this age, when a positive and warm world outlook can be arrived at through relaxation techniques, music and art, role-play, fairy tales, and space and freedom to choose.

There is a widespread perception in Perm that the atmosphere is ripe for a provision such as the health centres linked to schools' liberalisation, and perhaps, in particular, the power of the popular media to create a climate and culture of health awareness, through advertising and so on, have combined to create a 'market' for health, without the resources or the 'products' yet being available. As one course leader put it, 'we have the room, but where is the furniture?' This view was strongly echoed by a headteacher in the area, speaking at a day conference organised for the project, who spoke of the strength of family concerns about health, but the lack of state support. Disturbingly, she spoke too of the damaging effect of existing schooling structures on the psychological well-being of children; at her school, psychologists run workshops for teachers to offer guidance.

This refers us back to the concerns expressed about the current gap between the appetite for change, and actual school provision in terms of methodology, environment, and so on. This headteacher, a progressive, was open about the damage that she felt her children to be suffering within the existing structures of school provision in her school. For progress to quicken, a new development must be the use of pilot schools as key agents of change. This headteacher's school, impressively, is developing a culture of choice for teachers and students, about methodology, leisure time activities, classroom tasks etc.; the school also believes strongly in the value of parental involvement and a safe school environment. Discussions with teachers and observations of classes leave no doubt that this school is pioneering formidably strong approaches to the delivery of health education, and monitoring of its students' health – and that it is doing so while candidly admitting to the need to do more.

The potential is surely there for this school to act as a training provider to other schools within a consortium, perhaps with the school-based health centre as a starting point for this.

All of these are areas for expansion within the region of Perm. There remains the question of what the project members from the EU can now do to further and support the efforts of our colleagues in Russia. Beyond continuing to offer resources and research support, we can continue to provide access to models of school-based provision, both in the EU and through mobility visits to Perm from EU-based practitioners. For example, we have so far on this project hosted visits from six Perm-based course leaders, and taken two health education practitioners to Perm twice each.

This pattern will be continued but intensified in the course of the rest of 2001, with 15 visitors from Perm to EU partner countries. There will be course leaders, seeking to revise and develop course content, as well as, crucially, a number of practising school teachers, whose experience of schools in the EU countries may be influential in supporting efforts to introduce change in Perm. We also have a further six visitors from Perm in 2001, who will in all likelihood be key figures from the administration, and therefore central to the task of building an infrastructure within and beyond schools for the delivery of health education. Add to these a further week to be spent by our practitioners in Perm, working entirely in schools and with course members, and the emphasis on practitioner skills and practitioner exposure to international models is apparent.

The rich variety of experience on all these trips will surely offer plenty of ideas; though the partner countries show a marked convergence of thinking in all key areas, our approaches are inevitably dissimilar in detail and balance, and this provides a context for Perm-based discussion and development, when set alongside the distinct features of their own situation, which must ultimately dictate development.

Conclusions

In a 1998 volume of the series Oxford Studies in Comparative Education, *Processes of Transition in Education Systems*, in a piece edited by Elizabeth A. McLeish & David Phillips, a model is presented of the multiple phases of transition from totalitarian to democratic regimes, in political and economic structures. In Perm this year, the model was introduced for discussion. The model described the authoritarian phase, the anti-authoritarian phase, the period of ideological collapse, the time in which uncertainty prevails, periods of national policy formulation, phases of macro- and micro-level transitions, and so on. In discussion, it was concluded that Perm felt as though it was, in some ways, occupying all of these territories simultaneously! Understanding and accepting this notion, daunting on the surface, is in my view an essential part of the future of the project, as is the understanding that it has taken those of us working in the EU several generations of health education provision to arrive at the imperfect place in which we now stand.

The achievements of our colleagues in Perm are remarkable and incomplete, and we have now certain key foundation stones in place for the continued growth of the work of this project, over the next 18 months and beyond. First, we have nearly 5 years of shared international work in this field and in the field of special needs education, with all the goodwill that has accrued from this. Second, we have the continued support of the local administration, in financial, political, and organisational terms, a support which is to be continued for at least 4 more years. Third, we have an ever-increasing body of colleagues in Perm who are trained or who are in training as school-based coordinators of health education. Fourth, an increasing number of these colleagues are visiting EU countries to assess for themselves the approaches of the West to health education. Fifth, the resources room at PSPU is moving rapidly towards the point at which it can gain and offer access to the Internet, region-wide email, and so on, with all the advantages that this will bring. And sixth, colleagues in Perm are evaluating their own work, seeking to reflect on and change their own practice in the light of their experience and that of their students in schools.

As I have indicated, there remain big obstacles to progress, but there is also a massive impetus for progress, too. Certainly, it is a project in which the participants are optimists, and the energy and dedication that teachers, trainers, and children bring to their work in education cannot but augur well for the future. Patience is crucial, and a recognition that each step must be consolidated if the characterisation of Perm as a 'region of evergreen tomatoes' is to be challenged. The foundation stones being put in place at present will, it is to be hoped, provide a secure basis for sustained and inclusive change in the years to come.

Reference

McLeish, E.A. & Phillips, D. (Eds) (1998) *Processes of Transition in Education Systems*, Oxford Studies in Comparative Education (Wallingford, Triangle Books).

In Conclusion

JOHN SAYER

This concluding chapter draws on findings in the book, and dwells on policy and management issues of international projects, particularly in EU TEMPUS contexts. It contrasts the increasing reliance on target-related assessment and the application of inappropriate tools of accountability with the aspirations to extend experience, understandings, relationships and horizons in the new trans-European contexts. The encroachment of accountability mechanisms on professional responsibility and mutual confidence is seen as a symptom of a much more general malaise. In questioning the sharp division between EU development and research programmes, this concluding chapter examines the future role of universities in the new societies of Europe, and the value of comparative approaches to development at times of transition and change.

TEMPUS and Partnership

The TEMPUS-PHARE and TEMPUS-TACIS programmes, though franchised out, were initially the responsibility of the EC Task Force Unit for cooperation with third countries. The Head of Unit, Franz-Peter Küpper, expressed the aims of the programme as a base for new human relations with new human beings. He asserted that this is not an expert programme, but one of cooperation among experts. He saw its activity as learning together, the base for global understanding and a peace process.

That is an inspiring vision, and one which would have the assent of colleagues in all the countries involved. It contrasts with the pressure of immediate self-interests and missionary zeal which have been apparent in many west-east and east-west transactions in Europe. Transfer of 'know-how' or 'support' to 'beneficiaries' may have been what east European countries shedding a command economy were seeking in the very short term to fill a vacuum, and in what some west European national governments and enterprises have been most willing to invest.

But as east European countries have found themselves the dumping ground for goods, including intellectual goods which are surplus or unsellable in the home country, and dependent on processes which in any case may be unsuitable for transfer, such approaches can understandably cause disillusionment and anger, and be a barrier to understanding and sustained cooperation. It is often difficult to bring the rhetoric of cooperation among equals towards reality, or to find ways to work together which are likely to work beyond the life of funded projects.

Perm colleagues had identified these dangers before embarking on our projects, and saw clearly that those core activities which were to continue must be funded from within, whether by the University, the city or the region, that the international dimension should be seen as mutual enhancement, enrichment and learning experience. Models for successful change or transition are helpful as a common language through which to promote discourse, thought and progress, but as Alastair White points out, cannot be used as templates. The comparative approach adopted has not been to seek ideal models in lands of milk and honey, but to share issues, observe how they are tackled in a variety of situations, see ourselves as others see us, grow in self-understanding and then consider what in a particular context would be the most valuable and practicable approach. The general principles, drawn from our project by Ines Budnik, are of self-help, respect, faith, and contextual entirety.

That is not, however, what is being measured in accountability procedures which seek to ensure tangible products giving value for money. The criteria adopted for PHARE or TACIS projects whose specific objectives are predetermined by negotiation with recipient governments and then put out to tender are inadequate for TEMPUS proposals of interactive, largely voluntary exploration with longer term aspiration. Of course, prudent use of public money must be accounted for, but when this becomes the predominant mode of assessment, it takes over from and suppresses the Küpper vision, and reduces development to a previously identified minimum, whereas what we see at best in such projects is development beyond what could have been predicted.

Development and Research

Inter-university development programmes are more akin to research, and indeed, our experience suggests that they can best be promoted by research-based approaches. The questions are important, the outcomes may be hypothesised but cannot be known in advance; if they could, there would be no justification for the research. Many of our chapters are drawn from research studies facilitated by and informing the development project.

However, a TEMPUS development project is not intended or permitted to fund research. It may derive from research, or prompt research, and indeed is doing so, but TEMPUS will not pay for that, unless it is expressed as development or action. This limitation is very strange in view of the priorities of the EU for research and development as a whole, and its view of university-led projects as having the best hope of 'multiplying' to future leaders, spreading the effects of funding in priority areas.

Since the second EU research funding programme, 1994-98, there has been a new dimension of research cooperation with central and eastern Europe, and with developing countries, in accordance with article 130j of the Maastricht Treaty, which acknowledges that it may be appropriate to engage in international cooperation activities with international organisations and third countries other than the countries covered by the European Economic Area. Whilst no doubt the priorities of environment, energy, and health prompted this opening, it also applied to the small new area of funded socio-economic research, including research into education and training.

On the research side, there are signs that both the EU and national funding bodies are encouraging proposals which relate to applied projects; but there is no sign as yet of similar encouragement for development. The dichotomy between research and development is a false one artificially sustained by the separate funding mechanisms and criteria. Thereby, the mission of the university in Europe is called into question, particularly when in many European countries the institutional assessment of universities and the individual assessment of academics is bizarrely weighted away from teaching and social impact towards research publication per se. The danger is that inter-university development projects will be deprived of the highest quality research universities, especially given the very loose EU definition of a university as an institution following secondary education. Appropriate elements of research should be seen as instruments and/or products of development, relating personal, professional and institutional agendas, and thereby drawing on the full potential of those involved with the full encouragement of their universities.

Harmony of Central and Local Initiatives

Much is recorded in preceding chapters of the unusual degree of collaboration between the Perm State Pedagogical University and the city and region authorities of Perm. This is all the more remarkable given the control of the University not by regional but by the federal ministry 2000 kilometres away in Moscow. The local partnership has been again forged by personal relationships as well as formal Duma funding priority decisions. It has depended on individual commitment.

Personal relationship approaches to change are often accompanied by an inability to institutionalise developments. In this instance, the persons involved were also people with key political and institutional roles. It was a timely initiative: the Federal Government had in 1996 passed new education laws and guidelines with significant elements of human rights, access and parental choice, and the region had agreed its interpretation, with a major section on what we might identify as special needs. The framework for our project was Russian: what was sought was the kind of impetus this new project could bring, opening an international perspective to a geographically remote region and a city still finding its way from closed security to an exposed and uncertain future.

The strong commitment of city and region has not meant that all the proposals made during the project have been adopted, but it has meant they have been taken seriously, and issues of special need have become a priority. As is pointed out by one of the teachers interviewed, this may involve go-ahead individual pilot schools having to take a step backwards, when regulations are brought in which bring all schools some way forward in a coherent policy. That, as a project, we readily understand and accept, remembering how many years it has taken in other countries for new approaches to be assimilated, and knowing that future contexts are unpredictable for all of us. What has been important to our Russian colleagues is that the concepts of SEN – even if some of us are looking for other language – are becoming accepted instead of the strong tradition of defectology; and the profile of work with children having special needs is raised, and there is greater understanding and respect across the system and society as a whole.

Personal Links

Publications, such as this one and those created during the course of a project, are themselves an important development activity, and shared writing has been a feature of the Perm project. Six of our chapters are examples. Without personal relationships, management structures would be useless, and it is the spirit of a project much more than its technical construction which enables it to come and stay alive. Initial work has to be on shared vision, understandings, commitment, and mutual trust. The innovation in the TEMPUS-TACIS schemes of a pre-project year to formulate, indeed decide whether to proceed with, a full proposal was found to be particularly helpful, and it is to be regretted that this has now been withdrawn. Our second project, however, has been able to use the first for preliminary exploration, and this owes much to the more recent TEMPUS trend to build on successful previous initiatives.

Responsible or Accountable?

It is because of the importance attached to personal relationships, personal commitment and trust, and to the perceptions and feelings of teachers as explored in several of our chapters, that we have to return to management issues related to accountability and professional responsibility.

A project founded on trust, commitment and the principle of public service must have an element of congruity in the management of the scheme as a whole. From a project which has been judged positively both on its own criteria and by those applied externally, we have a duty to insist without fear of whinging that the scheme within which we operate should be congruous with a partnership approach. As coordinator, too much of my time has been taken as a shock-absorber between a practice of control by fear and trusting partnership. Professional freedom is a hard-earned and necessary condition. It comes with responsibility to the public, to learners, to fellow actors and to the exercise of professional judgement. Responsibility is positive and enabling. It is what draws us into education. It is what we expect of ourselves and what is expected of us. Professional freedom and responsibility aspire to the highest standards, to excellence.

Accountability, on the other hand, is presented as a means of public protection, but is predominantly a means of control. It drags educators down from self-responsibility. It is based on fear, whereas teaching is based on love. Accountability measures by minimum standards. It is a dead hand, deficiency-oriented. Where is the space for high aspiration? Accountability could be justified, in cases where projects appear not to be meeting required standards; but is not the right measuring rod for all. Yes, there must be fair ways to counter incompetence. But there is a danger of the wheel-tapper checking and hearing the constant dud sound of cracked wheels, without realising it is the hammer which is cracked. In the decade in which it has been my privilege to direct TEMPUS projects, there has been a serious deterioration of trust and relationship between projects and the scheme as a whole, now dominated not by shared professional appraisal but by all-absorbing one-way financial scrutiny. That trend, in public services generally in and amongst European countries, has to be reversed, if active and responsible citizenship is to thrive. The best way we can achieve that is by insisting on underlying values and engaging in such activities despite all.

This is not just a TEMPUS problem. In Britain, and England in particular, education and health services are being subjected to the same misconceived incentives and threats (league tables, cash rewards for good institutions). Carrot and stick measures are alien and ineffective for caring professions. The problem is not confined to Britain. In international development programmes, the European Commission with its agencies has been forced, by fear of criticism, away from creating space for new opportunities to the misapplication of management by objectives and proceduralistic accountability, shooting itself in the foot. Western societies are in danger of replicating east European subservience before the Iron Curtain came down; we have been busy fencing ourselves in.

Professional freedom has its problems, too. Educators are never satisfied with themselves. Professional freedom and responsibility take on the requirements of learners and their future, and transmute these into learning opportunities. We can live with that if we have the space to aspire; stress is caused by outside interference, imposition of minimalist external requirements, breakdown of trust and confidence. It has been a privilege to coordinate a group drawn from four countries and institutions with a common professional concern and commitment to worthwhile learning.

Notes on Contributors

Ines Budnik is Lecturer in the Department for Education, Martin-Luther Universität, Halle-Wittenberg.

Sacha van der Greft is a research student and project assistant at the University of Amsterdam.

Evgeni Khenner is Professor and Chair of the Department of Computer Science, Perm State Pedagogical University.

Alexei Kniazev is a leader specialist in the Computer Centre, Perm State Pedagogical University.

Andrei Kolesnikov is Rector, Perm State Pedagogical University.

Andrea Laczik is a research officer and TEMPUS project assistant, University of Oxford Department of Educational Studies.

Olga Leontieva is a research student, Faculty of Computer Science, Perm State Pedagogical University.

David Martin is an international consultant, and doctoral researcher, University of Amsterdam.

Gudrun Meister is an assistant, Centre for School and Teacher Research, Martin-Luther Universität, Halle-Wittenberg.

Anna Popova is an interpreter from Perm State Pedagogical University, currently undertaking doctoral studies at the University of Birmingham.

John Sayer is a tutor and TEMPUS Projects Director, 1991-2000, University of Oxford Department of Educational Studies, Professor h.c., Perm State Pedagogical University.

Dmitri Tchoulakov is a doctoral research lecturer in Social Policy, Perm State Pedagogical University.

Hartmut Wenzel is Dean and Professor of Education, Martin-Luther Universität, Halle-Wittenberg.

Alastair White has been a tutor and TEMPUS project director, 2000-, University of Oxford Department of Educational Studies, and is now Deputy Head, Cheney School, Oxford.

Kees van der Wolf is Professor of Education, University of Amsterdam.

Yana Yemboulaeva is a research student in the Faculty of Foreign Languages, Perm State Pedagogical University.